# WASHINGTON TRIVIA

Bob
for Christmas '01
from Nancy, John
Kendal-Hilary

# WASHINGTON TRIVIA

COMPILED BY PATRICIA CALLANDER HEDTKE
AND JOHN V. HEDTKE

Rutledge Hill Press®
*Nashville, Tennessee*
*A Thomas Nelson Company*

Published by Rutledge Hill Press, a Thomas Nelson Company, P.O.
Box 141000, Nashville, Tennessee 37214.

*Typography by Bailey Typography, Nashville, Tennessee*

**Library of Congress Cataloging-in-Publication Data**

Hedtke, Patricia Callander, 1952–
    Washington trivia / compiled by Patricia Callander Hedtke and
John V. Hedtke.
      p. cm.
    ISBN 1-55853-137-8
    1. Washington (State)—Miscellanea. 2. Questions and answers.
I. Hedtke, John V.  II. Title.
F891.5.H43  1991
979.7'0076—dc20

                                       91-34089
                                         CIP
Printed in the United States of America

4 5 6 7 8—05 04 03 02 01

# PREFACE

There is certainly a lot more to be said about the state of Washington than is covered in this small volume, but, knowing the people of Washington, when the time is right, it will be said.

I would like to thank Vonda N. McIntyre, for putting us in touch with Rutledge Hill Press, the librarians at the University of Washington's Suzallo Library, and the librarians at both the Sno-Isle and Seattle Public Library Systems for all their help tracking down information. I would also like to thank Brian Goldade for the information only a native could give me, Brian Schiffer for his sports knowledge, and Ted Cook, Ann Mittelstaedt, Leon Reed, Gordon Goodykoontz, and Traepischke Graves for their help with entertainment questions. Thanks also to Ruby Montana's Pinto pony for props. And I offer a special thanks to Jayne Patterson for introducing me to what I think was the funniest bit of trivia.

May the Spirit of Tahoma forever watch over us all.

PCH, June 1991

To my mother, Lucille Rose Smith
—PCH

# TABLE OF CONTENTS

# GEOGRAPHY

## CHAPTER ONE

**Q.** What is the only state named after a U.S. president?

**A.** Washington.

———◆———

**Q.** What is nearly twice the size of Rhode Island and has about seven thousand residents?

**A.** The Yakima Indian Reservation.

———◆———

**Q.** What is the center of Lake Washington's Gold Coast?

**A.** Meydenbauer Bay in Bellevue.

———◆———

**Q.** What Washington town was planned to be the Pittsburgh of the West?

**A.** Kirkland.

———◆———

**Q.** Apple Tree Cove on the Kitsap Peninsula was given its name because of what mistake?

**A.** The flowering dogwoods were thought to be apple trees.

Q. Of the four cities in the world named Walla Walla, where are the three outside Washington?

A. Australia.

---◆---

Q. Some people say that the town of George was not named for the president, but for what?

A. The founder's dog, George.

---◆---

Q. What geological formations that chart the geologic history of the region are seen at Palouse Falls?

A. Layers of basaltic lava.

---◆---

Q. Who discovered the Enchantments Lakes about thirty years ago?

A. Peg and Bill Stark.

---◆---

Q. What historic site is now buried under Lake Roosevelt?

A. Kettle Falls.

---◆---

Q. Snohomish County is a sister county with what area in Japan?

A. Ishikara.

---◆---

Q. What town was named for a battle that did not take place?

A. Battle Ground.

**Q.** What oral historian is trying to get official recognition for the Pacific Northwest Trail?

**A.** Ron Strickland.

◆

**Q.** In Okanogan County, what do Tough Nut, Wooloo Mooloo, War Eagle, and Johnny Boy have in common?

**A.** They are all mines.

◆

**Q.** What is the largest sand spit on earth?

**A.** Dungeness.

◆

**Q.** What was Bellingham once called?

**A.** New Whatcom.

◆

**Q.** What two places in Washington have earned the name Graveyard of the Pacific?

**A.** The mouths of the Strait of Juan de Fuca and the Columbia River.

◆

**Q.** For whom was the town of Nahcotta named?

**A.** Chief Nahcati.

◆

**Q.** What is the name of Washington's youngest mountain range, which is only about two million years old, one of the youngest in the world?

**A.** The Olympic.

**Q.** What is Ballard's nickname?

**A.** Snoose Junction.

---◆---

**Q.** At 5,595 feet, what is the highest mountain pass in Washington?

**A.** Sherman.

---◆---

**Q.** How many acres of national forest are in Washington?

**A.** Nine million.

---◆---

**Q.** What city in Washington was originally a Hudson Bay Company outpost in 1825?

**A.** Vancouver.

---◆---

**Q.** What percentage of land is privately owned in Washington?

**A.** Fifty percent.

---◆---

**Q.** What do Mounts Olympus and Dryad have in common besides their Greek names?

**A.** Both are located on the Olympic Peninsula.

---◆---

**Q.** What city is named after a region described in the Bible as rich in fruit?

**A.** Ephrata.

Q. What is Washington's leading fishing port?

A. Westport.

◆

Q. What underlies all the prairies around Puget Sound?

A. Gravel from Ice Age glaciers.

◆

Q. What is the area of Washington?

A. 68,129 square miles, making it the twentieth largest state.

◆

Q. What connects two peninsulas and thirteen islands and is the largest of its kind in North America?

A. The Washington State Ferry System.

◆

Q. What city is the self-proclaimed bicycling capital of the Northwest?

A. Redmond.

◆

Q. What city is Washington's beef capital?

A. Ellensburg.

◆

Q. What is the most likely date it will be a sunny day in the Puget Sound?

A. July 26.

**Q.** What three Washington counties have the lowest electric rates in the country?

**A.** Chelan, Douglas, and Grant.

---

**Q.** What city has the highest number of Ph.D's?

**A.** Richland.

---

**Q.** What is the largest U.S. island in Puget Sound?

**A.** Whidbey.

---

**Q.** What Washington city is the self-proclaimed logging capital of the world?

**A.** Forks.

---

**Q.** What county has both the westernmost and northwesternmost points in the continental United States?

**A.** Clallam.

---

**Q.** Historically, what is Longview's claim to fame?

**A.** It was the West's first planned city.

---

**Q.** Where was the first European settlement in Washington?

**A.** Fort Nunez Gaona at Neah Bay (1792).

Q. What Washington county has the smallest population and lowest crime rate?

A. Garfield.

———— ✦ ————

Q. What Washington community is known as Little Norway?

A. Poulsbo.

———— ✦ ————

Q. Where is the oldest operating sawmill west of the Mississippi River?

A. Port Gamble.

———— ✦ ————

Q. Where was the world's largest pumpkin (612 pounds) grown?

A. Chelan.

———— ✦ ————

Q. How many counties are in Washington?

A. Thirty-nine.

———— ✦ ————

Q. What was the name of Washington's "phantom county"?

A. Ferguson.

———— ✦ ————

Q. What Washington city has the world's record for snowfall in a single season?

A. Paradise (93.5 feet).

Q. What county has coastlines on both the Pacific Ocean and Puget Sound?

A. Jefferson.

———◆———

Q. What is the deepest gorge in North America?

A. Hell's Canyon (over 5,000 feet deep) in Asotin County.

———◆———

Q. What has its surface 1,100 feet above sea level and its bottom 400 feet below sea level?

A. Lake Chelan.

———◆———

Q. What county has the largest area and the fewest people per mile in the state?

A. Okanogan.

———◆———

Q. What is the nickname of Pacific County's courthouse in South Bend?

A. Gilded Palace of Reckless Extravagance.

———◆———

Q. What county in Washington became the state's first nuclear-weapons-free zone?

A. San Juan.

———◆———

Q. What county is both the smallest and totally unreachable by road?

A. San Juan.

**Q.** What city boasts the second largest skywalk system in the United States?

**A.** Spokane.

---

**Q.** What lake runs the length of Stevens County and then into Canada?

**A.** Lake Roosevelt.

---

**Q.** What is the largest U.S. river to flow north?

**A.** The Pend Oreille.

---

**Q.** Where is the world's largest single hop field?

**A.** Toppenish (1,836 acres).

---

**Q.** In what two crops does Yakima lead the country?

**A.** Mint and apples.

---

**Q.** What three cities make up the Tri-Cities?

**A.** Kennewick, Pasco, and Richland.

---

**Q.** What was Galloping Gertie's official name?

**A.** The Tacoma Narrows Bridge.

Q. What county changed its name from Slaughter because the residents did not like it?

A. Kitsap.

◆

Q. What islands bear the Spanish name of the Greek explorer Apostolos Valerianos?

A. San Juan de Fuca.

◆

Q. Other than having been presidents, what do Adams, Garfield, Grant, Jefferson, Lincoln, and Pierce have in common?

A. They gave their names to counties in Washington.

◆

Q. What town was given a Spanish-sounding name to increase its real estate prospects?

A. Anacortes.

◆

Q. What Cascade community was once called Squak?

A. Issaquah.

◆

Q. What city is known as the Atomic City?

A. Richland.

◆

Q. What town was damaged by Tusko the elephant on May 15, 1927?

A. Sedro Woolley.

Q. What two mountain ranges can be seen from Seattle?

A. The Cascades and the Olympics.

———◆———

Q. What is the nation's longest lava tube cavern?

A. Ape Cave.

———◆———

Q. What is the second largest river in North America?

A. The Columbia.

———◆———

Q. What city is known as the City of Destiny?

A. Tacoma.

———◆———

Q. Which four of the San Juan Islands have regular Washington state ferry service?

A. Lopez, Shaw, Orcas, and San Juan.

———◆———

Q. What Washington city was named after a railroad car manufacturer?

A. Pullman.

———◆———

Q. What city decked itself out as a Bavarian village to draw tourists?

A. Leavenworth.

———◆———

Q. Besides Washington, what were the three other suggested names for the state?

A. Tahoma, Columbia, and Washingtonia.

Q. What is the cartographic nickname for El Gran Canal de Nuestra Senora del Rosario la Marina?

A. Rosario Strait.

———◆———

Q. What was the name Sir Francis Drake gave to the Pacific Northwest, including Washington, in 1579?

A. Nova Albion.

———◆———

Q. What county has one town and less than two thousand people?

A. Garfield.

———◆———

Q. What was Seattle's original name?

A. Duwamps.

———◆———

Q. What is the city with the highest altitude in Washington?

A. Waterville (2,640 feet).

———◆———

Q. What city is known as the Apple Capital of the World?

A. Wenatchee.

———◆———

Q. What is the most photographed mountain in the world?

A. Mount Shuksan.

Q. What did President Millard Fillmore do in 1853 for the Pacific Northwest?

A. He created the federal territory of Washington.

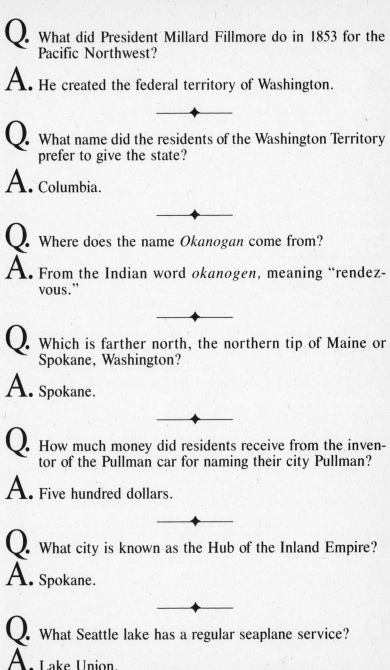

Q. What name did the residents of the Washington Territory prefer to give the state?

A. Columbia.

Q. Where does the name *Okanogan* come from?

A. From the Indian word *okanogen,* meaning "rendez-vous."

Q. Which is farther north, the northern tip of Maine or Spokane, Washington?

A. Spokane.

Q. How much money did residents receive from the inventor of the Pullman car for naming their city Pullman?

A. Five hundred dollars.

Q. What city is known as the Hub of the Inland Empire?

A. Spokane.

Q. What Seattle lake has a regular seaplane service?

A. Lake Union.

Q. What is the correct pronunciation of the Pend Oreille River?

A. PAHN-do-RAY.

---

Q. Before refrigeration, where did the Mount Adams area residents get their ice?

A. From the Ice Caves.

---

Q. What community is known as the Antique Capital of the Northwest?

A. Snohomish.

---

Q. What do the Queets, Quinalt, and Hoh forests have in common?

A. They each get about twelve feet of rainfall every year.

---

Q. What National Historic District was once called Little Venice because it was built around so many creeks and streams?

A. Skamakawa.

---

Q. Which city is known as the Emerald City?

A. Seattle.

---

Q. What was the Klickitat name for Mount Saint Helens?

A. *Tah-one-lat-clah* or "mountain of fire."

Q. What is Washington's top tourist attraction?

A. Puget Sound.

———◆———

Q. What part of Washington has been described as "a unique collection of non-soils"?

A. The Tacoma tide flats.

———◆———

Q. How many sites in Washington have been designated as superfund clean-up sites by the Environmental Protection Agency?

A. Thirty-four.

———◆———

Q. In 1981, the year that Tacoma opened its public fishing pier on Commencement Bay, what warning about it was issued?

A. Fishermen should not eat cancerous fish from the bay.

———◆———

Q. What part of Washington is losing fourteen tons of topsoil per acre each year primarily because of runoff?

A. The Palouse.

———◆———

Q. What was Ellensburg's early name?

A. Robber's Roost (after its first store).

———◆———

Q. When Mount Saint Helens blew up, the ash cloud was so thick that the street lights went on in what town?

A. Yakima.

Q. Who gave the name *Palouse*, meaning "lawn," to the region?

A. Early French fur traders.

———◆———

Q. At 450 miles east of the Pacific Ocean, what is Washington's most inland seaport?

A. Clarkston.

———◆———

Q. Where is Washington's Banana Belt?

A. The islands in the Strait of Juan de Fuca.

———◆———

Q. What is the name of the rock formation in the middle of the Spokane River at Riverside Park in Spokane?

A. The Bowl and Pitcher.

———◆———

Q. What is the name of the warm ocean current that keeps the coastal waters free from ice?

A. The Japanese Current.

———◆———

Q. In 1936, what lodge so impressed President Franklin D. Roosevelt with its surrounding forest that he pushed through the creation of the Olympic National Park?

A. Lake Quinalt Lodge.

———◆———

Q. How much taller is Snoqualmie Falls than Niagara Falls?

A. One hundred feet.

**Q.** What do Seattle and Rome have in common geographically?

**A.** Both are built on seven hills.

———◆———

**Q.** How old is the Cascade Mountain Range?

**A.** About twenty-five million years.

———◆———

**Q.** What does *Spokane* mean?

**A.** "Children of the sun" or "the sun people."

———◆———

**Q.** How did early settlers try to determine the depth of Elliott Bay?

**A.** By tying a horseshoe to a rope and dropping it overboard.

———◆———

**Q.** When glaciers covered the Northwest, how thick was the ice in the Seattle area?

**A.** Four thousand feet.

———◆———

**Q.** Which of the Tri-Cities is known as a river trade port?

**A.** Kennewick.

———◆———

**Q.** What Ice Age remnant of the Columbia River is 3½ miles long and 600 feet high?

**A.** Dry Falls.

Q. What is the current name of the mountain that was named El Cerro de la Santa Rosalia by Juan Perez in 1774?

A. Mount Olympus.

——◆——

Q. What was the nickname of Wenatchee, referring to its geographic location?

A. The Buckle of the Pacific Northwest Power Belt.

——◆——

Q. What was carved out of sixty miles of rock by an ice movement?

A. Lake Chelan.

——◆——

Q. What is the most remote resort community in the United States?

A. Stehekin.

——◆——

Q. What is the top tourist attraction in central Washington?

A. Grand Coulee Dam.

——◆——

Q. Why did Seattle raise the streets after the great fire of 1889?

A. To keep the toilets from backing up when the tide came in.

——◆——

Q. Though not as full of minerals as the Great Salt Lake, what Washington lake has a reputation for buoyancy?

A. Soap Lake.

Q. When was most of downtown Spokane built?

A. 1880–1940.

◆

Q. What country declared the Haro Strait as the dividing line between the United States and what is now Canada?

A. Germany.

◆

Q. What created the Puget Sound?

A. A glacier.

◆

Q. How many ethnic pioneer groups left their mark on the state?

A. Three (Spanish, English, and American).

◆

Q. How many freezing nights does Spokane usually have each year?

A. 138.

◆

Q. When the glacial dam holding prehistoric Lake Missoula in northern Idaho crumbled, what do geologists say stopped the most tremendous flood in the New World from reaching the Pacific Ocean?

A. The Cascade Range.

◆

Q. Although "Fifty-four Forty or Fight" was James K. Polk's 1844 presidential campaign slogan, the boundary between Washington and Canada was fixed at what latitude by the 1846 Treaty of Oregon?

A. Forty-ninth parallel.

Q. When one flies east out of Sea-Tac International Airport, which side of the plane allows a close-up view of Mount Rainier?

A. The right (south).

———◆———

Q. What explorer named more Washington sites than any other?

A. Lt. Charles Wilkes.

———◆———

Q. What do old Conconully, Loomis, and Molson have in common?

A. All are ghost towns in Washington.

———◆———

Q. What is found one hundred feet below the wheat lands of central Washington?

A. Volcanic lava.

———◆———

Q. What is another name for the Columbia River?

A. Wauna.

———◆———

Q. What is the name of the legendary mountain bridge that spanned the Columbia Gorge?

A. Tahmahnaw.

———◆———

Q. In which county do the Snake and the Columbia, the two great rivers of Washington, merge?

A. Franklin.

Q. What Washington island is named for a Fijian headman captured by the Wilkes expedition?

A. Vendovi Island.

---

Q. What is the affectionate name given to people from Bellingham?

A. Bellinghamsters.

---

Q. How long is Washington's Pacific coastline?

A. 157 miles.

---

Q. What went into creating the Channeled Scablands?

A. Lava flows and Ice Age flooding.

---

Q. What is the most unusual rock formation found within the Spokane city limits?

A. Columnar palisades.

---

Q. What is the highest waterfall in the state?

A. Ferry Falls (701 feet).

---

Q. What are the names of the two phantom islands in the San Juans mapped by the Wilkes expedition?

A. Adolphus and Gordon.

Q. The Olympic Peninsula was a part of what prehistoric South Sea island?

A. Wrangellia.

———◆———

Q. Which Washington city is the westernmost town in the contiguous forty-eight states?

A. La Push.

———◆———

Q. The community of Bingen has a sister city in what other country?

A. Germany.

———◆———

Q. Near what city were the first European grape vines planted?

A. Kennewick.

———◆———

Q. Along what Washington river is over one hundred miles of rivers and beach?

A. The Snake River.

———◆———

Q. Where is the "home of Granny Smith apples"?

A. Douglas County.

———◆———

Q. What dam is the highest in the Northwest?

A. Mossyrock (606 feet).

**Q.** What Washington city elects an official grouch each year?

**A.** Kettle Falls.

———————◆———————

**Q.** What Washington city was named by its founder for a supposed survivor of the lost continent of Atlantis?

**A.** Orondo.

———————◆———————

**Q.** What Washington city is the site of a monument commemorating three Soviet flyers who pioneered the transpolar air route?

**A.** Vancouver.

———————◆———————

**Q.** Where were the "fanciful" lighthouses of eastern Washington situated?

**A.** On the Palouse.

———————◆———————

**Q.** Napa North and Fruit Bowl of the Nation are names given to what Washington area?

**A.** The Yakima Valley.

———————◆———————

**Q.** In his retirement, Juan de Fuca told tales of finding the legendary Strait of Anian, inspiring explorers to seek what nonexistent route?

**A.** The Northwest Passage.

———————◆———————

**Q.** What Seattle park was once the private estate of Guy Phinney?

**A.** Woodland.

Q. What two other states considered the name *Washington* but decided against it?

A. Minnesota and Mississippi.

---

Q. What is happening to the Paradise Ice Caves near Mount Rainier?

A. They are melting.

---

Q. John S. McMillan founded which "harbor" in the San Juans?

A. Roche.

---

Q. What telephone company serves the Washington town of Point Roberts?

A. The British Columbia Telephone Company.

---

Q. What travel book classed Spokane as a small city and refused to include Richland?

A. *Exploring Washington's Smaller Cities.*

---

Q. What eastern Washington town was left off the state's official highway map?

A. Wilbur.

---

Q. What city is known as the City of Smokestacks?

A. Everett.

Q. Where is Mile-High Hurricane Ridge?

A. The Olympic National Park.

———◆———

Q. What city is named for a potato?

A. Wapato.

———◆———

Q. What nickname, currently used by Alaska, was originally applied to the Olympic Peninsula?

A. America's Last Frontier.

———◆———

Q. The admission of Washington to the union as a state also
commemorated what other event?

A. The centennial celebration of George Washington's inau-
guration.

———◆———

Q. Before the name was changed to the San Juan Islands,
what was the official name?

A. The San Juan Archipelago.

———◆———

Q. What state imports 99 percent of its fresh milk from
Washington?

A. Alaska.

———◆———

Q. What is the tallest treeless mountain in the world?

A. Rattlesnake Mountain (3,560 feet).

Q. What three counties make up Panoramaland?

A. Ferry, Stevens, and Pend Oreille.

---◆---

Q. What Washington city takes its name from a play by Shakespeare?

A. Othello.

---◆---

Q. What Washington town shipped a twenty-two-ton lump of coal to the 1893 Chicago World's Fair?

A. Roslyn.

---◆---

Q. For whom was Clarkston named?

A. William Clark (of the Lewis and Clark expedition).

---◆---

Q. What San Juan island is known as the Yankee Go Home island?

A. Shaw.

---◆---

Q. What is the inscription on the Washington side of the Blaine Peach Arch?

A. "Children of a Common Mother."

---◆---

Q. Where is the second largest marina on the West Coast?

A. Everett.

**Q.** Where is Washington's oldest public square?

**A.** Downtown Vancouver.

———◆———

**Q.** Where is the only ocean beach airstrip in the nation?

**A.** Copalis Beach.

———◆———

**Q.** When were the first pictures of Washington taken from space?

**A.** April 1960 (by TIROS).

———◆———

**Q.** What modern trail follows the roadbed of the Seattle, Lake Shore, & Eastern Railroad?

**A.** The Burke-Gilman Trail.

———◆———

**Q.** What county is called the mother of Washington counties?

**A.** Lewis.

———◆———

**Q.** Where did the Kalispel Indians worship?

**A.** Manresa Grotto.

———◆———

**Q.** What Washington airport has part of its runway in Canada?

**A.** Laurier.

Q. What city began as a mission of Dr. Marcus Whitman?

A. Walla Walla.

---

Q. Where is the only park in Washington established primarily for whale watching?

A. Lime Kiln Whale Watch State Park on San Juan Island.

---

Q. Where does the Oregon Trail technically end?

A. Fort Vancouver, Washington.

---

Q. What is the highest point in the San Juan Islands?

A. Mount Constitution.

---

Q. Which side of Mount Saint Helens blew off?

A. The north side.

---

Q. What two towns claim to be in the exact center of the state?

A. Wenatchee and Ellensburg.

---

Q. What Bellingham Bay settlement was founded by smuggler Dirty Dan Harris?

A. Fairhaven.

Q. According to a poll in *Washington Magazine*, what are the top three waterfalls, as decided by waterfall lovers, in the state?

A. Palouse Falls, Spray Falls, and Falls Creek Falls.

———◆———

Q. What well-known local landmark is a couple of miles north of Chehalis?

A. The Hamilton Farms billboard.

———◆———

Q. By what name was Liberty Bay formerly known?

A. Dog Fish Bay.

———◆———

Q. What mnemonic sentence do Seattlites use to remember the names of the streets downtown?

A. "Jesus Christ Made Seattle Under Protest."

———◆———

Q. What resort community was named after a town in Switzerland?

A. Lucerne.

———◆———

Q. What town was named by spelling the name of a Washington governor backwards?

A. Retsil (Gov. Ernest Lister).

———◆———

Q. What town, formerly named Goat Creek, was renamed with the Spanish word for "mountain goat"?

A. Mazama.

**Q.** Who named the town of Olympia?

**A.** Col. Isaac Ebey.

---

**Q.** What is distinctive about the Long Beach Peninsula?

**A.** It is the longest natural beach in the U.S.

---

**Q.** What is the Roza Flow?

**A.** It is the largest known prehistoric lava flow (over fifteen thousand square miles).

---

**Q.** What city has the most single men and women in the state?

**A.** Pullman.

---

**Q.** How many "James Islands" are there in Washington?

**A.** Two (one near La Push and the other near Decatur Island in the San Juans).

---

**Q.** How much rain does the Yakima Valley receive per year, on the average?

**A.** About seven inches.

---

**Q.** What town (now disincorporated) in Whitman County once held the world's largest prune dryer?

**A.** Elberton.

Q. What unusual act of courtship did Captain George Davidson perform for Ellinor Fauntleroy?

A. He named mountains for her, her sister, and her brothers (Mount Ellinor, Mount Constance, and The Brothers).

———◆———

Q. What town was once named "Saluskin" in honor of Chief Saluskin of the Yakima Indians?

A. Harrah.

———◆———

Q. What town was once disincorporated by the Atomic Energy Commission?

A. Richland.

———◆———

Q. What town was named for a vice president of the Northern Pacific Railroad?

A. Lamont (Daniel Lamont).

———◆———

Q. What is the world's largest oyster hatchery?

A. The Coast Oyster Company (in Quilcene).

———◆———

Q. What is the northernmost U.S. town on the Columbia River?

A. Northport.

———◆———

Q. What did the Oregon Territorial Legislature change Vancouver County into on September 3, 1849?

A. Clark County.

Q. What town was once named Slaughter in honor of Lt. William A. Slaughter, a casualty of the Indian War of 1855–56?

A. Auburn.

◆

Q. How was Beacon Rock formed?

A. It was originally the core of a volcano.

◆

Q. What town was named with the Indian word for "whirlwind" because of the dust devils in the area?

A. Moxee City.

◆

Q. What town's name, sometimes reported as having been the number of a locomotive, a boxcar, or a survey station, probably came from the Chinook word for "fork" or "junction"?

A. Tenino.

◆

Q. What town supposedly derives its name from a contraction of "Hell-to-pay"?

A. Eltopia.

◆

Q. Other than the incorporated town of Woodland in Cowlitz County, how many unincorporated communities in Washington are named Woodland?

A. Four.

◆

Q. What hot springs' name directly translates as "Oh, look!"?

A. Ohanapecosh Hot Springs.

# ENTERTAINMENT

## C H A P T E R   T W O

**Q.** What Seattle-born vaudeville star tossed a garter belt into the orchestra pit at the Ziegfeld Follies?

**A.** Gypsy Rose Lee.

◆

**Q.** What television personality telephoned Bruce Nelsen, then president of the Washington Association of Pea and Lentil Producers, to ask what a lentil is?

**A.** David Letterman.

◆

**Q.** Who were the Seattle women about whom the television series "Here Come the Brides" was loosely based?

**A.** The Mercer girls.

◆

**Q.** What is the most famous fictitious town in Washington?

**A.** Twin Peaks.

◆

**Q.** Where is one of the largest sound stages outside of Los Angeles?

**A.** Pacific Northwest Studios in Seattle.

Q. What favorite son of South Bend launched his 1968 presidential campaign on the Smothers Brothers television show?

A. Pat Paulsen.

◆

Q. What name did Herman Brix use in more than 140 films?

A. Bruce Bennett.

◆

Q. What Tacoma native has made belts for stars on "Dynasty" and "Hotel"?

A. Cynthia Warden.

◆

Q. What popular children's television show with a nautical theme aired in Spokane?

A. "Captain Cy."

◆

Q. What country music superstar got her start at the Delta Grange Hall in Whatcom County and soon started singing at a tavern in Blaine?

A. Loretta Lynn.

◆

Q. What Seattle native has been the singing voice for such stars as Audrey Hepburn and Natalie Wood?

A. Marnie Nixon.

◆

Q. What Washington child prodigy won the Old Time Fiddle championship at the age of twelve?

A. Mark O'Connor.

Q. Who wrote *The Mount Saint Helens Symphony*?

A. Alan Hovhaness.

◆

Q. What Paul Newman movie did cinematographer James Wong Howe have to his credit?

A. *Hud*.

◆

Q. World-famous dancer Abdullah Jaffa Anver Bey Kahn is better known by what name?

A. Robert Joffrey.

◆

Q. What prompted Dorothy Bullitt, owner of KING Broadcasting Company, to first buy a television station?

A. An article in *Life* magazine.

◆

Q. Bruce Lee's wife, Linda Emery, was a former homecoming queen for which high school in Seattle?

A. Garfield.

◆

Q. At age seventeen, what Spokane soprano became the youngest singer signed by the Metropolitan Opera?

A. Patrice Munsel.

◆

Q. What was the name of the Colfax native who supervised the chariot race in Charlton Heston's *Ben Hur*?

A. Yakima Canutt.

Q. What was the name of the entrepreneur who began his multimillion dollar theater chain in Seattle?

A. Alexander Pantages.

---

Q. What Seattle native worked on Disney's *Fantasia*?

A. Henry ("Hank") Ketcham.

---

Q. Before becoming mayor of Seattle, what did Charles Royer do at KING-TV?

A. He was a commentator.

---

Q. In what capacity did Washingtonian Maurice Seiderman work for Orson Welles for twelve years?

A. As his personal make-up man.

---

Q. What Washington native starred as a white-clad reporter in the television show, "The Night Stalker" (later known as "Kolchak")?

A. Darren McGavin.

---

Q. What former Tacoma resident became known for her role as the oldest daughter in the television series "Father Knows Best"?

A. Elinor Donahue.

---

Q. Seattle's businesses were the first in the country to pipe what into their shops?

A. Muzak.

Q. What movie began with an assassination at the top of the Space Needle?

A. *Parallax View.*

———◆———

Q. What popular singing group of the 1950s took their name from an Olympia telephone exchange?

A. The Fleetwoods.

———◆———

Q. What event was the first television broadcast in Seattle?

A. A high school football game.

———◆———

Q. Where did the 1984 world premiere of the film *Greystoke* take place?

A. Central Washington University.

———◆———

Q. Craig T. Nelson, star of the television series "Coach," hails from what Washington city?

A. Spokane.

———◆———

Q. What "Saturday Night Live" personality hails from eastern Washington?

A. Julia Sweeney.

———◆———

Q. What former *Seattle Times* music critic founded the *Earshot Jazz Newsletter*?

A. Paul de Barros.

Q. The Spokane-based National Music Service offers special music programs to what kind of business?

A. Funeral homes.

◆

Q. What movie starred Robert Mitchum tromping around in the snows of Mount Rainier?

A. *Track of the Cat.*

◆

Q. What movie about Bigfoot was filmed in the Seattle area?

A. *Harry and the Hendersons.*

◆

Q. What two popular movies of the 1980s were shot in Tacoma?

A. *I Love You to Death* and *Three Fugitives.*

◆

Q. What city in Washington has the largest movie-going population in the country?

A. Seattle.

◆

Q. What Washingtonian starred in the serial "Tarzan and the Green Goddess," also released as "The New Adventures of Tarzan"?

A. Herman Brix ("Bruce Bennett").

◆

Q. A collection of Bing Crosby memorabilia is found where?

A. The Crosby Library at Gonzaga University in Spokane.

**Q.** Where did the Beatles stay when they played in Seattle?

**A.** The Edgewater Inn.

———◆———

**Q.** What Washington singer/dancer starred in *All That Jazz*?

**A.** Ann Reinking.

———◆———

**Q.** What song did the Mothers of Invention write about fishing from the window of their room at the Edgewater Inn?

**A.** "Mudshark."

———◆———

**Q.** What movie was filmed partially on the Whidbey-Port Townsend ferry *Kulshan*?

**A.** *An Officer and a Gentleman.*

———◆———

**Q.** Where were the cartoons found on the "J. P. Patches Show"?

**A.** In his hat.

———◆———

**Q.** Who was Brakeman Bill's puppet companion?

**A.** The Crazy Donkey.

———◆———

**Q.** Washington native Craig T. Nelson starred in what Steven Spielberg movie?

**A.** *Poltergeist.*

Q. Where is Jimi Hendrix's grave?

A. Greenwood Memorial Park Cemetery in Renton.

◆

Q. Who gave one of the largest Christmas parties in history?

A. The Boeing Company, in 1979 (103,152 employees and families).

◆

Q. What Yakima-born actor appeared in *Dune*, *Blue Velvet*, *The Doors*, and played the part of FBI Agent Cooper in the TV series "Twin Peaks"?

A. Kyle MacLachlan.

◆

Q. What famous crooner was a native of Tacoma?

A. Bing Crosby.

◆

Q. What Robert De Niro movie used Mount Baker as the scenery?

A. *The Deer Hunter*.

◆

Q. What Oscar-winning director left Hollywood to live in Washington?

A. Stanley Kramer.

◆

Q. What was the name of the Bremerton native whom Ida Lupino married?

A. Howard Duff.

Q. What Washington singer and dancer is best known for her role in *Hello, Dolly?*

A. Carol Channing.

———◆———

Q. Where is the television show "Northern Exposure" filmed?

A. Roslyn.

———◆———

Q. What was the real name of the person portrayed as Jason Bolt on the television series "Here Come the Brides"?

A. Asa Mercer.

———◆———

Q. What entertainer from Walla Walla became the Caped Crusader on television?

A. Adam West.

———◆———

Q. What was the motto of guitar-playing restaurateur Ivar Haglund?

A. Keep Clam.

———◆———

Q. What Washington-born rock musician ended his 1967 Monterey Pop Festival performance by burning his guitar?

A. Jimi Hendrix.

———◆———

Q. What folksinger wrote songs for the Bonneville Power Administration to promote public power?

A. Woody Guthrie.

Q. What was the name of the Elvis Presley movie set at the 1962 Seattle World's Fair?

A. *It Happened at the World's Fair.*

◆

Q. What animal rights activist and game show host is from Darrington?

A. Bob Barker.

◆

Q. What former Puget Sound newscaster became a famous national network anchorman?

A. Chet Huntley.

◆

Q. What Washington native did Jessica Lange play in the movie *Frances*?

A. Frances Farmer.

◆

Q. Where did KING-TV news anchorman Mike James go to college?

A. Washington State University.

◆

Q. What popular singer and musician was born in Everett?

A. Kenny Loggins.

◆

Q. Where is the oldest operating movie theater in Washington?

A. Roslyn.

**Q.** Where was the first season of the television show "Twin Peaks" filmed?

**A.** Snoqualmie.

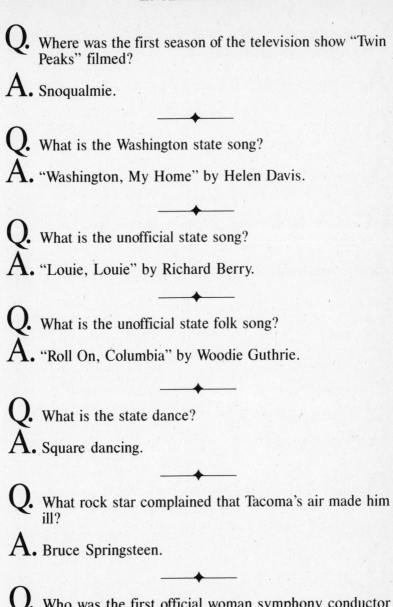

**Q.** What is the Washington state song?

**A.** "Washington, My Home" by Helen Davis.

**Q.** What is the unofficial state song?

**A.** "Louie, Louie" by Richard Berry.

**Q.** What is the unofficial state folk song?

**A.** "Roll On, Columbia" by Woodie Guthrie.

**Q.** What is the state dance?

**A.** Square dancing.

**Q.** What rock star complained that Tacoma's air made him ill?

**A.** Bruce Springsteen.

**Q.** Who was the first official woman symphony conductor in the world?

**A.** Madame Mary Davenport Engberg (conductor of the Bellingham Symphony Orchestra).

Q. Both the Beach Boys and the Kinks recorded what beloved Washington song?

A. "Louie, Louie."

◆

Q. What Washington musician has billed himself as the World's Most Obscure Rock Star?

A. Jef Jaisun.

◆

Q. What song mentions over thirty Washington cities in its lyrics?

A. "Godzilla Ate Tukwila."

◆

Q. What type of performance is Kent Stowell's *Seattle Slew*?

A. A ballet.

◆

Q. What is considered the greatest hit of the Brothers Four?

A. "Green Fields."

◆

Q. What popular song, recorded by Bing Crosby and the Andrews Sisters, was written by Washingtonians John Rarig and Dixie Lou Thompson?

A. "Black Ball Ferry Line."

◆

Q. What complete operatic cycle was mounted in both English and German at the Seattle Opera House annually from 1975 to 1983?

A. *Der Ring des Nibelungen.*

Q. Phi Gamma Delta fraternity at the University of Washington gave birth to what famous singing group?

A. The Brothers Four.

———◆———

Q. What is the name of the Salish and Nootka spiritual leader and traditional singer who has kept alive such songs as "The Traveling Canoe Song" and "The Welcome Song"?

A. Johnny Moses.

———◆———

Q. Who wrote the song "The Frozen Logger"?

A. James Stevens.

———◆———

Q. Although Ralph Chaplin wrote "Solidarity Forever" in Chicago, who brought the song to national attention?

A. Striking Puget Sound loggers.

———◆———

Q. Stoddard King is best known for what popular song of World War I?

A. "There's a Long, Long Trail."

———◆———

Q. The song "Dog and Butterfly" sent the name of what Washington rock group to the top of the charts?

A. Heart.

———◆———

Q. Who recorded the theme song "Seattle" for the television show "Here Come the Brides"?

A. Perry Como.

Q. What nationally syndicated radio show features Washington songs and poems in a segment entitled "The Upper Lefthand Corner"?

A. Sandy Bradley's "Potluck."

◆

Q. "Walk (Don't Run)" was a hit tune for what group?

A. The Ventures.

◆

Q. To what name did the popular bar band Seafood Mama switch when they hit it big?

A. Quarterflash.

◆

Q. After a 1929 performance at Yakima's Capitol Theater, what cowboy singer added his signature to the backstage graffiti?

A. Gene Autry.

◆

Q. Who made the two-ton, twenty-three-foot wind harp situated at Agate Pass?

A. Ron Konzak.

◆

Q. "Come Softly to Me" was a hit song for what Olympia-based singing group?

A. The Fleetwoods.

◆

Q. The success of the rock-and-roll band Heart rests on the music-writing ability of what two sisters?

A. Ann and Nancy Wilson.

Q. Edward Curtis made a film in 1914 about the Kwakiutl Indians that was restored and re-released under what title?

A. *In the Land of the War Canoes.*

◆

Q. What is the motto of the Flying Karamazov Brothers?

A. We Juggle Till We Drop.

◆

Q. What did labor organizer Jack Walsh create to get people's attention?

A. A street band.

◆

Q. What was the name of Geoff Hoyle's one-man performance at the Seattle Repertory Theatre?

A. *Feast of Fools.*

◆

Q. Written by Judge Francis Henry in 1874, what song became Ivar Haglund's theme song and the source of a restaurant's name?

A. "The Old Settler" (also known as "Acres of Clams").

◆

Q. What former Spokane *Spokesman Review* columnist has been called the "most plagiarized poet in the United States"?

A. Stoddard King.

◆

Q. Under what name did Don McCune appear on television?

A. Captain Puget.

Q. Uncle Torval, Aunt Torval, and Chef Sam Samoto were the alter egos of what children's show performer?

A. Stan Boreson.

———◆———

Q. What Woodie Guthrie song tells of migrant workers coming to the Northwest?

A. "Pastures of Plenty."

———◆———

Q. What jazz musician is known to her fans as the Avant Goddess?

A. Amy Denio.

———◆———

Q. What is the vocation of the members of the Strange Attractors blues band?

A. They are all physicists.

———◆———

Q. Who is the principal ballerina of the Pacific Northwest Ballet?

A. Deborah Hadley.

———◆———

Q. To what Seattle research institute is Bob Hope's name attached?

A. The Bob Hope Heart Research Institute.

———◆———

Q. What cultural landmark did the town of Twisp once have?

A. An opera house.

Q. What song about a Washington clam was a hit in Japan and Australia?

A. "The Gooey Duck Song."

✦

Q. Friday Harbor was portrayed in what 1966 movie?

A. *Namu the Killer Whale*.

✦

Q. Forest Service employee Rob Jeter built a baby grand piano on the top of what mountain?

A. Mount Bonaparte.

✦

Q. What is the name of the largest banjo club in Washington?

A. Seattle Banjo Club.

✦

Q. What Seattle songwriter wrote the score for *Lady and the Tramp* at Disney Studios?

A. Oliver Wallace.

✦

Q. As the Sun Valley Trio, Washington songwriters Tafft Baker, Larry Prise, and Charles Macak wrote and popularized what song?

A. "The Hokey-Pokey."

✦

Q. What national radio commentator announced on his program in 1985 that the Skagit Valley tulips were not blooming?

A. Paul Harvey.

Q. What was the theme song for the "Klubhouse Show" with Stan Boreson?

A. "Zero Dacus."

◆

Q. Who is the host of KING-TV's satirical "Almost Live"?

A. John Keister.

◆

Q. At what age did jazz performer Ronny Whyte leave Seattle?

A. Eighteen.

◆

Q. Who wrote the novelty tune "Friendly Neighborhood Narko Agent"?

A. Jef Jaisun.

◆

Q. What alumnus of Evergreen State College created the hit television show, "The Simpsons"?

A. Matt Groening.

◆

Q. What actor, best-known for playing Cliffie the Mailman on the television show "Cheers," recently moved to Washington and has set up a business selling ecologically safe packing materials?

A. John Ratzenberger.

◆

Q. Who is considered to be the world's greatest spoon player?

A. Artis the Spoon Man.

Q. What Jack Nicholson movie was filmed in the San Juans?

A. *Five Easy Pieces*.

---◆---

Q. How much was Woodie Guthrie paid for the songs he wrote popularizing public power?

A. $266.66.

---◆---

Q. For what type of music is singer Diane Schuur noted?

A. Jazz.

---◆---

Q. Who are the musical accompanists for Sandy Bradley, host of the nationally syndicated radio show "Potluck"?

A. The Small Wonder String Band.

---◆---

Q. What movie starring Michael Douglas and Kathleen Turner prominently features the Flying Karamazov Brothers?

A. *The Jewel of the Nile*.

---◆---

Q. What famous magician leaped while manacled into the Spokane River in 1910?

A. Harry Houdini.

---◆---

Q. Tacoma's Pantages Theater was the site for the 1940 premier of what Ronald Reagan movie?

A. *Tugboat Annie Sails Again*.

Q. What film was named for the first bomber, a Boeing plane, to complete twenty-five missions from England in World War II?

A. *Memphis Belle.*

—◆—

Q. How many years was Stan Boreson's "KING's Klub-house" on television?

A. Twelve.

—◆—

Q. What famous bandmaster said that Spokane and Walla Walla had excellent audiences?

A. John Phillip Sousa.

—◆—

Q. When was the first motion picture shown in the state?

A. 1896.

—◆—

Q. What Seattle native was portrayed by Linda Hunt in *Waiting for the Moon*?

A. Alice B. Toklas.

—◆—

Q. Who owned the first piano in the state?

A. Richard and Ann Covington (in 1850).

—◆—

Q. What Disney movie featured the Omak Stampede and Suicide Race?

A. *Run, Appaloosa, Run.*

**Q.** Bainbridge mystery writer Aaron Elkins created the character Dr. Gideon Oliver, who was played by what actor on the ABC Monday Mystery Movie?

**A.** Lou Gossett, Jr.

---

**Q.** In what artistic medium does Spokane resident Christopher Aponté work?

**A.** Dance.

---

**Q.** What former host of "Almost Live" is now the host of "The Match Game"?

**A.** Ross Schafer.

---

**Q.** What Washington theater was the first to produce the Michael Frayn comedy *Noises Off*?

**A.** Centre Stage.

---

**Q.** What play was a huge success in Seattle but did not make it onto Broadway?

**A.** *Angry Housewives*.

---

**Q.** A school candy sale gone wrong is the theme for what movie shot in Kirkland?

**A.** *The Chocolate War*.

---

**Q.** What Cornish Institute student composed *The Cantata for Beltane*?

**A.** James Gagné.

Q. Aerial views of both Grant and Lincoln counties are featured in what Mel Gibson and Goldie Hawn movie?

A. *Bird on a Wire.*

---◆---

Q. What is western Washington's most requested comedy rerun?

A. "Mr. Ed."

---◆---

Q. What are the two favorite filming locations in Seattle?

A. The Pike Place Market and Pioneer Square.

---◆---

Q. What 1976 Connie Stevens movie was set in Washington?

A. *Scorchy.*

---◆---

Q. What was the only radio station in the country to hook up with Armed Forces Radio in Saudi Arabia during the Persian Gulf Crisis?

A. KXRX.

---◆---

Q. Who is Seattle's favorite television news anchorperson?

A. Jean Enersen.

---◆---

Q. What is the name of a four-act opera based on the native American experience in Puget Sound?

A. *Songs from the Cedar House.*

Q. "Queen of the Reich" was a hit for what Washington heavy metal band?

A. Queensryche.

◆

Q. What is the name of the largest gay men's choir in the United States?

A. Seattle Men's Chorus.

◆

Q. Thelma Young's Second City Dance Theater evolved into what eastern Washington dance troupe?

A. The Spokane Ballet.

◆

Q. What is the largest film festival in Washington?

A. The Seattle International Film Festival.

◆

Q. In the 1920s, what city in Washington had more theaters than any other city north of San Francisco?

A. Bellingham.

◆

Q. What movie featured John Wayne as a member of the Seattle Police Department?

A. *McQ*.

◆

Q. Matthew Broderick played a Seattle teenager in what movie?

A. *War Games*.

Q. Aerial shots of Seattle were used in what Bill Cosby movie?

A. *Ghost Dad.*

---

Q. Where is the Nez Perce Music Archive containing nearly 800 songs from 1897 to the present?

A. Washington State University.

---

Q. What Michael Weller play premiered in Seattle?

A. *Soapy Smith.*

---

Q. For what type of production is Spokane's Civic Theater famous?

A. Musicals.

---

Q. Samuel and Israel Goldfarb's "My Dreydl" was adopted by what school district to sing during Hanukkah?

A. Seattle Public Schools.

---

Q. In what movie did Debra Winger track a killer to the Puget Sound but could not get anyone to believe her?

A. *Black Widow.*

---

Q. What "Dallas" star went to Cascade High School in Everett and trained at the University of Washington?

A. Patrick Duffy.

**Q.** What Washington theater company received the 1980 Jenny Heiden Award?

**A.** The Young ACT Company.

◆

**Q.** What is the setting for the play *The Longest Walk*?

**A.** Chief Seattle's grave.

◆

**Q.** What Edmonds area musician is best known for his contemporary acoustic guitar playing?

**A.** Eric Tingstad.

◆

**Q.** Pam and Philip Boulding, who are internationally famous for making and playing Celtic harps, are better known by what name?

**A.** Magical Strings.

◆

**Q.** What famous movie of the 1930s starring Clark Gable was shot in Washington?

**A.** *Call of the Wild.*

◆

**Q.** How long has the Total Experience Gospel Choir been around?

**A.** More than a decade.

◆

**Q.** Which member of the group Mannheim Steamroller lives in Seattle?

**A.** Chip Davis.

Q. Which one of Janet Thomas's plays won the Empty Space Theater's Northwest Playwright's Competition in 1978?

A. *Heads and Tails.*

◆

Q. What actress who lives on the Puget Sound plays Ruthann, the manager of the general store in the television show "Northern Exposure"?

A. Peg Phillips.

◆

Q. What county's commissioners voted to support changing the state song to "Louie, Louie"?

A. Whatcom.

◆

Q. What city was the backdrop for *The Fabulous Baker Boys*?

A. Seattle.

◆

Q. What internationally known blues singer and guitar player was born and raised in Tacoma?

A. Robert Cray.

◆

Q. What actress, who formerly played Marcie on "All My Children," is now a media coordinator in Issaquah?

A. Doreen Seely.

◆

Q. What movie set in Washington starred Dick Van Dyke as a priest?

A. *The Runner Stumbles.*

**Q.** What banjo player, formerly living in Seattle and now living in the Palouse, is equally famous for his classical and his minimalist jazz banjo playing?

**A.** Paul Smith.

◆

**Q.** What actor, raised in Washington, has appeared on television and in such movies as *The Beastmaster* and *If You Could See What I Hear*?

**A.** Marc Singer.

◆

**Q.** What movie with Sidney Poitier featured shots of the Seattle freeway?

**A.** *The Slender Thread.*

◆

**Q.** Washingtonians Brian Andrew, Vic Trier, and Lyle Carpenter all have what vocation in common?

**A.** Elvis impersonation.

◆

**Q.** What actor, who appeared in *M.A.S.H.*, *Poltergeist III*, *Alien*, *Top Gun*, and *Steel Magnolias*, lives in the San Juans?

**A.** Tom Skerrit.

◆

**Q.** What singer of folk and popular songs grew up in Washington?

**A.** Judy Collins.

◆

**Q.** What was the site used as Divine's home in the film *Trouble in Mind*?

**A.** The Seattle Art Museum.

Q. What was the name of the musical written to officially commemorate the Washington territorial centennial?

A. *Eliza and the Lumberjack.*

◆

Q. Seattle was the location for the world premiere of what John Pielmeir play that later became a movie starring Jane Fonda?

A. *Agnes of God.*

◆

Q. What movie that led to a television series for Bill Bixby was shot in Washington?

A. *The Magician.*

◆

Q. Who wrote "Hallelujah, I'm a Bum"?

A. Haywire Mac McClintock.

◆

Q. What Grammy-award winning jazz artist opened her own club in Seattle?

A. Ernestine Anderson.

◆

Q. What was the first national music hit written and produced in the Northwest?

A. "Hindustan."

◆

Q. Seattle's University district was the site for the running scene in what Patty Duke movie?

A. *Before and After.*

Q. What member of the Brothers Four is now a KOMO newscaster?

A. Dick Foley.

———————◆———————

Q. Righteous Mothers, Dos Fallopia, and Motherlodge have what in common?

A. They sing women's music.

———————◆———————

Q. What Warren Beatty and Julie Christie movie was set in Washington during the Gold Rush?

A. *McCabe and Mrs. Miller.*

———————◆———————

Q. In Gary Iwamoto's play *Twinkle*, what city is the main character said to be from?

A. Bellevue.

———————◆———————

Q. Con artists and con games are major themes of what movie shot in Seattle?

A. *House of Games.*

———————◆———————

Q. What Steve Martin movie was filmed in British Columbia but was set in Washington?

A. *Roxanne.*

———————◆———————

Q. The lecture scene in the George C. Scott movie *The Changeling* was shot where?

A. The University of Washington.

Q. Jami Seiber of Rumors of the Big Wave plays what unusual instrument?

A. Electric cello.

---◆---

Q. What Peter Fonda movie had Idaho's name in it but was shot in Redmond?

A. *Idaho Transfer.*

---◆---

Q. What instrument does Port Townsend resident Bud Shank play?

A. Alto sax.

---◆---

Q. What radio station that bills itself as the "Jazz Giant" once refused to co-sponsor a concert featuring Ornette Coleman?

A. KPLU.

---◆---

Q. Rose Louise Hovick was the original name of what Washington-born entertainer?

A. Gypsy Rose Lee.

---◆---

Q. What Tacoma disc jockey is internationally famous for his show "Jazz after Hours"?

A. Jim Wilke.

---◆---

Q. Dayton author Robert Shields wrote the novel *The Reno Gang*, which was developed into what Elvis movie?

A. *Love Me Tender.*

# HISTORY

## C H A P T E R   T H R E E

Q. When you are called to be a juror in the Municipal Court in Seattle, who explains to you (on videotape) the responsibilities of being a juror?

A. Perry Mason (Raymond Burr).

◆

Q. Who was instrumental in getting Oysterville included on the National Register of Historic Places?

A. Dale Espy Little.

◆

Q. At what time did the 6.5-level earthquake hit Seattle on April 29, 1965?

A. 8:29 A.M.

◆

Q. For what wrongdoing was the first automobile owner in Clark County cited?

A. Not tying his car to a hitching post.

◆

Q. What bank, founded by Dorsey Syng Baker, is Washington's oldest bank?

A. The Baker–Boyer National Bank.

Q. What long-time Spokane resident was thought by some to be the outlaw Butch Cassidy?

A. William T. Phillips.

———————◆———————

Q. Who was elected as mayor of Seattle in 1926, thereby becoming the first woman mayor of a large American city?

A. Bertha Landes.

———————◆———————

Q. What Washingtonian won the 1976 Massachusetts Democratic presidential primary?

A. Henry M. ("Scoop") Jackson.

———————◆———————

Q. What Washington businessman was dubbed by *Newsweek* magazine "the Diaper King"?

A. David Abrams, founder of Baby Diaper Service.

———————◆———————

Q. Chehalis' McKinley Stump, built for a whistle-stop speech by President McKinley, was actually used for the first time by what president?

A. Theodore Roosevelt.

———————◆———————

Q. Who almost destroyed the boomtown of Everett in the 1890s by withdrawing all of his investments in the area?

A. John D. Rockefeller.

———————◆———————

Q. What was the name of the Iron Man of the Hoh, who could easily carry a cast-iron stove?

A. John Huelsdonk.

**Q.** What started the Spokane fire of 1889?

**A.** Pork chop grease.

---

**Q.** After the devastating fires of 1889, with what material did the cities of Spokane, Ellensburg, and Seattle rebuild?

**A.** Brick.

---

**Q.** What museum houses a 104-year-old collection of Women's Christian Temperance Union records?

**A.** The Cheney Cowles Memorial Museum in Spokane.

---

**Q.** What Midwest agitator, who introduced the term *hatchetation*, was presented with a deed to a building lot in Spokane's Hollywood addition?

**A.** Carry Nation.

---

**Q.** What is the real name of the two-room "Ma and Pa Military Museum" on a ranch in Moses Lake?

**A.** Scheffner Military Museum.

---

**Q.** Where was the headquarters of the Bicentennial Reality Party, whose Raw Deal platform was committed to selling votes and allowing special interests to pay for certain laws?

**A.** Tukwila.

---

**Q.** When the ARCO *Anchorage* ran aground, creating the worst oil spill in Puget Sound history, what was cited as the cause?

**A.** Pilot error.

Q. What famous sea captain doubted the existence of the Strait of Juan de Fuca when he saw nothing at that latitude?

A. Captain James Cook.

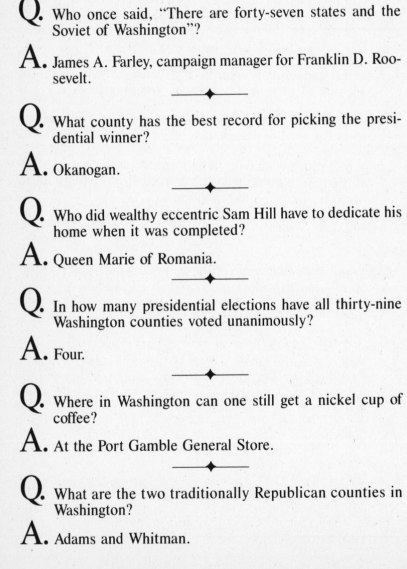

Q. Who once said, "There are forty-seven states and the Soviet of Washington"?

A. James A. Farley, campaign manager for Franklin D. Roosevelt.

Q. What county has the best record for picking the presidential winner?

A. Okanogan.

Q. Who did wealthy eccentric Sam Hill have to dedicate his home when it was completed?

A. Queen Marie of Romania.

Q. In how many presidential elections have all thirty-nine Washington counties voted unanimously?

A. Four.

Q. Where in Washington can one still get a nickel cup of coffee?

A. At the Port Gamble General Store.

Q. What are the two traditionally Republican counties in Washington?

A. Adams and Whitman.

**Q.** Where was Jimmy Carter when he learned he had lost the 1980 presidential election?

**A.** At Sea-Tac International Airport.

---

**Q.** Who organized the state's first Women's Christian Temperance Union chapter in Colfax?

**A.** Lucy Messer.

---

**Q.** What Tacoma lawyer often criticized President Eisenhower for being too liberal?

**A.** His older brother, Edgar Eisenhower.

---

**Q.** The Washington State Society, founded in 1961, is situated in what city?

**A.** Washington, D.C.

---

**Q.** What is the name of the oldest sailing vessel in Puget Sound, which first operated as a North Sea fishing vessel over ninety years ago?

**A.** The *Sylvia*.

---

**Q.** What early mayor of Port Townsend disappeared (and has never been found) January 14, 1917?

**A.** Israel Katz.

---

**Q.** Supporters of what former senator were known as "Maggie's Boys"?

**A.** Warren Magnuson.

Q. What position did Richard Nixon's younger brother, Edward, hold at the University of Washington?

A. Navy instructor for the ROTC.

---◆---

Q. What public figure called the Washington taxpayer "Joe Sixpack"?

A. Governor Booth Gardner.

---◆---

Q. When did the Washington state flag appear on a U.S. stamp?

A. In 1976 (on a bicentennial commemorative).

---◆---

Q. What ethnic group was at the forefront of the cannery labor movement in the 1930s?

A. Filipinos.

---◆---

Q. What ethnic group was expelled from Seattle and Tacoma in the mid-1880s?

A. The Chinese.

---◆---

Q. Along with the Amish and the Mennonites, what Washington Anabaptist sect can trace its roots directly to the Protestant Reformation?

A. The Hutterites.

---◆---

Q. What Washington U.S. senator ordered the capitol police to arrest and bring in two senators in order to fill a quorum?

A. Brock Adams.

**Q.** What Chinese contractor helped rebuild Seattle after the fire of 1889?

**A.** Chin Jee Hee.

---

**Q.** In what direction is George Washington turned toward on the Washington state flag?

**A.** Toward his right.

---

**Q.** From what resource is Washington's Clean Water fund derived?

**A.** A tax on tobacco.

---

**Q.** To what did the term *pearldiver* refer in the Pacific Northwest in the 1890s?

**A.** An itinerant dishwasher.

---

**Q.** Wenatchee was the touchdown point for what historic forty-two-hour flight?

**A.** The first nonstop flight from Japan to the United States.

---

**Q.** What is the name of the family-owned railroad that runs from Kennewick to Yakima?

**A.** The Washington Central Railroad.

---

**Q.** What single parent inspired his oldest daughter, Sonora, to lobby for the creation of Father's Day?

**A.** William Jackson Smart.

Q. Who was Washington's first governor?

A. Elisha P. Ferry.

———◆———

Q. Who said, "All men were made by the Great Spirit Chief. They are all brothers. The earth mother is the mother of all people, and all people should have equal rights upon it"?

A. Chief Joseph of the Nez Perce.

———◆———

Q. Who was awarded the Martin Luther King, Jr., Award for Civic and Professional Achievement and was the first woman executive of the Seattle Urban League?

A. Rossalind Woodhouse.

———◆———

Q. Who bailed out over southwest Washington after completing the first and only successful hijacking of an American airliner?

A. D. B. Cooper.

———◆———

Q. What Seattle store is world famous for its selection of windup Godzillas, rubber slugs, pink flamingos, and glow-in-the-dark dinosaurs?

A. Archie McPhee.

———◆———

Q. What is the source of the "Tacoma aroma"?

A. Tacoma's many mills and other industries.

———◆———

Q. The majority of American lawyers trained in Japanese law were educated at what school?

A. The University of Washington.

**Q.** What is the average age of the members of the Washington Women's Christian Temperance Union chapter?

**A.** Seventy-nine.

---

**Q.** What was the landmark achievement of Washingtonian May Arkwright Hutton in 1912?

**A.** First woman delegate to the Democratic National Convention.

---

**Q.** In 1858, who established Saint Joseph's Hospital in Vancouver, the Northwest's first hospital?

**A.** Esther ("Mother Joseph") Pariseau.

---

**Q.** When did Washington become a territory?

**A.** March 2, 1853.

---

**Q.** What Seattle firm was the forerunner of the United Parcel Service?

**A.** American Messenger Company.

---

**Q.** What Nisei's case before Judge Voorhees helped to get Congress to compensate World War II Japanese–American detainees?

**A.** Gordon Kiyoshi Hirabayashi.

---

**Q.** What archbishop had his views on reproductive rights and family dynamics investigated by the Vatican?

**A.** Raymond Hunthausen.

**Q.** The Seattle Police Department became the first in the nation to put what kind of patrol squad on the streets?

**A.** Bicycle cops.

---

**Q.** What person made famous by the Watergate investigation is from Washington?

**A.** John Erlichman.

---

**Q.** Whose flagship led the parade through the Chittenden Locks when they were opened in 1917?

**A.** Commodore Matthew Perry.

---

**Q.** What British statesman was heard to say, "Monstrous, absolutely monstrous!" after he was searched by U.S. Customs in Seattle?

**A.** Winston Churchill.

---

**Q.** In what town was a pair of antique ice skates found?

**A.** The ghost town of Molson.

---

**Q.** On what date did Lewis and Clark return to Washington after their exploratory mission?

**A.** October 11, 1805.

---

**Q.** What is the oldest building still standing in the state?

**A.** A church built by John Clinger in Claquato in the late 1800s.

Q. What native American tribe is fighting to halt development in the elk wintering grounds in the foothills of Mount Rainier?

A. The Muckleshoot tribe.

————◆————

Q. What president signed legislation on October 2, 1968, to create the North Cascades National Parks Complex?

A. Lyndon Johnson.

————◆————

Q. The Yacolt fire that burned several hundred thousand acres killed how many people?

A. Thirty-eight.

————◆————

Q. The Spokane chapter of the Sons of Italy (Lodge 2172) held out until 1990 to comply with what national organizational change?

A. The admission of women.

————◆————

Q. Who owns the Space Needle?

A. Pentagram Corporation.

————◆————

Q. Who is the biggest single Washington Lotto winner to date?

A. Sandra Vaver ($13.5 million).

————◆————

Q. Since its inception in 1982 until mid-1991, approximately how much has the Washington Lottery taken in and paid out?

A. Approximately $1,843,000,000 taken in and $874,000,000 paid out.

Q. What was a big problem in the logging country in the 1930s?

A. Log rustling.

———◆———

Q. Who was the first registered guest of the Hotel Washington?

A. President Theodore Roosevelt.

———◆———

Q. What landmark of the Wild West, made famous by Mae West in the 1930s, can be found at Third and Washington in Seattle?

A. Diamond Lil's whorehouse.

———◆———

Q. What serial killer hailed from Washington?

A. Ted Bundy.

———◆———

Q. Who was Seattle's first Chinese pioneer?

A. Chun Ching Hock.

———◆———

Q. Who built Spokane House, the first trading post in the state?

A. Finan McDonald and Jacques Finlay.

———◆———

Q. During the Great Depression, what town's wooden scrip was the only one approved by the comptroller of the United States?

A. Tenino.

**Q.** The design for the state flag, adopted in 1923, was based on a design submitted in 1915 by what group of people?

**A.** The Daughters of the American Revolution.

---

**Q.** Who built the oldest house in Tumwater?

**A.** Capt. Nathaniel Crosby III (Bing's grandfather).

---

**Q.** What was the first Washington commercial product shipped to San Francisco?

**A.** Logs for pilings.

---

**Q.** Where is a typical fort from the days of Washington's Indian wars?

**A.** Fort Simcoe on the Yakima Indian Reservation.

---

**Q.** Where did the United States and England almost go to war over a pig?

**A.** English Camp.

---

**Q.** Where does the Seattle fishing fleet dock?

**A.** The Ballard Marina.

---

**Q.** What resident of Mount Saint Helens was quoted as saying shortly before the eruption, "If this damn thing takes this mountain, I'm going along with it."

**A.** Harry Truman (not the former president).

Q. The lower Yakima Valley is the heartland of what Washington industry?

A. Table wine.

———◆———

Q. What is written on the side of La Conner's police car?

A. La Conner La Police Le Car.

———◆———

Q. How well do Washington's wines sell in the United States?

A. Second only to California's.

———◆———

Q. Which fort did Hawaiian Islanders help staff for the Hudson Bay Company in 1825?

A. Fort Vancouver.

———◆———

Q. What was the native American language of commerce along the Columbia River?

A. A simplified version of Chinookan.

———◆———

Q. In 1860, the Bureau of Indian Affairs built the first boarding school for children on what reservation?

A. Yakima.

———◆———

Q. What four Civil War generals served in Washington before the war?

A. George B. McLellan, Winfield Scott, Isaac Stevens, and Ulysses S. Grant.

**Q.** What is the name given to the unknown perpetrator of the largest unsolved serial murder case in the country, with forty-nine known victims?

**A.** The Green River Killer.

---

**Q.** What is Washington's oldest seafood restaurant?

**A.** The Olympia Oyster House.

---

**Q.** Where was the site of the Great Depression's first Hooverville?

**A.** Where the Kingdome now stands in Seattle.

---

**Q.** On the average, how long did it take settlers to travel to Tumwater from Independence, Missouri?

**A.** Nineteen months.

---

**Q.** When Indira Gandhi visited Pasco in 1962, at what college did she lecture?

**A.** Columbia Basin College.

---

**Q.** What was the original use of the Old Hotel in Othello?

**A.** It was the county bordello.

---

**Q.** What classic children's toy did Walla Walla's Strausser Bee Supply Company first market?

**A.** Lincoln Logs.

Q. What Washington port handles more cargo than Seattle?

A. Tacoma.

---◆---

Q. Where is moored a full-sized replica of the ship that Capt. Robert Gray used to explore the Washington coast?

A. Aberdeen.

---◆---

Q. What Washington county was officially renamed to honor Martin Luther King, Jr., in 1986?

A. King.

---◆---

Q. Who was the first person to ship Washington timber to the Orient?

A. British explorer John Meares.

---◆---

Q. What association angered Washington vintners when they served only California and Italian wines at a gala dinner for one thousand guests?

A. The Restaurant Association of Washington State.

---◆---

Q. What is the Washington state ship?

A. The *President Washington* (a container vessel).

---◆---

Q. In which part of Washington did George Washington's descendant, Confederate soldier Bushrod Corbin Washington, settle at the turn of the century?

A. Grand Coulee.

Q. What was Boeing's first passenger plane, and when was it produced?

A. The 707, in 1958.

◆

Q. What is the oldest operating store in Washington?

A. The Tillinghast Seed Company in La Conner (opened in 1885).

◆

Q. Where did Japan Airlines train its 747 pilots?

A. Grant County Airport.

◆

Q. In what aspect of mining did Washington lead the country in the late 1800s?

A. Mining fatalities.

◆

Q. Who claimed the title King of Fidalgo Island?

A. William Munks.

◆

Q. Sen. Phil Talmadge was once fired by what Seattle law firm?

A. Karr Tuttle Campbell.

◆

Q. The King County prosecuting attorney's office was the first in the country to form what special unit?

A. A sexual assault unit.

**Q.** A company founded in Spokane by Gary Norton revolutionized banking with what device?

**A.** The electronic bank teller.

---

**Q.** Founded in 1934, what is the oldest gay bar in the United States?

**A.** The Double Header in Seattle.

---

**Q.** What Toppenish native served as superintendent of Indian affairs under President McKinley?

**A.** Estell Rell Myer.

---

**Q.** What was the name of the first Russian to defect in a Washington shopping mall?

**A.** Dmitri Vinogredov.

---

**Q.** Who was called in to settle the Pig War?

**A.** Emperor Wilhelm I of Germany.

---

**Q.** Who was the first woman executive director of the Washington Association of Wheat Growers?

**A.** Nedra Bayne.

---

**Q.** What was the name of the fleet of passenger steamships that served small Puget Sound communities in the early 1900s?

**A.** The Mosquito Fleet.

**Q.** What was the most important "employee benefit" at early Washington logging camps?

**A.** A good cook.

---◆---

**Q.** How much did Frederick Weyerhaeuser pay per acre for the first 900,000 acres he bought from the Northern Pacific Railroad?

**A.** Six dollars.

---◆---

**Q.** What happened to the Hood Canal Bridge on February 13, 1979?

**A.** It sank into the Hood Canal.

---◆---

**Q.** What was the source of the picture of George Washington that appears on the Washington state seal?

**A.** An advertisement for Dr. Jane's Cure for Coughs & Colds.

---◆---

**Q.** What Washington governor served only one day in office?

**A.** Samuel Cosgrove (in 1909).

---◆---

**Q.** What was the name of the Shoshone woman who was the interpreter for Lewis and Clark?

**A.** Sacajawea.

---◆---

**Q.** Of the approximately $200,000,000 in gold that came out of the Alaska gold rush, how much is estimated to have stayed in Seattle?

**A.** $100,000,000.

Q. How many of Washington's governors have died in office?

A. Three.

---

Q. What Washington politician was almost picked as John F. Kennedy's vice presidential running mate?

A. Henry M. ("Scoop") Jackson.

---

Q. What judge made the controversial 1974 Indian Fishing Rights decision?

A. George Boldt.

---

Q. For what Seattle financial institution's ad campaign was the "happy face" invented?

A. University Federal Savings and Loan Association.

---

Q. Who was the first woman to serve on the Washington state supreme court?

A. Judge Carolyn Dimmick (in 1981).

---

Q. What was the postmark for mail sent from the Seattle World's Fair in 1962?

A. Space Needle, WA.

---

Q. What Burlington Northern Railroad property blew up in 1980?

A. The top of Mount Saint Helens.

**Q.** What position did Congressman Brock Adams fill for the Carter administration?

**A.** Secretary of Transportation.

◆

**Q.** How many justices are there in the Washington state supreme court?

**A.** Nine.

◆

**Q.** What Washington kidnapping victim later gave a job to his kidnapper?

**A.** George Weyerhaeuser.

◆

**Q.** Who was the first black settler in Washington and the first settler ever in the Tumwater area?

**A.** George Washington Bush (in 1845).

◆

**Q.** What started a fifteen-hour fight in Rockport on May 16, 1973?

**A.** Tim Roetman drove a cement truck over a group of motorcycles.

◆

**Q.** What law did Skamania County pass regarding Bigfoot?

**A.** It became illegal to hunt it.

◆

**Q.** Where is the Nez Perce leader Chief Joseph buried?

**A.** Nespelem, in the Colville Reservation.

Q. Who attended the sixtieth anniversary rededication of the Maryhill Museum?

A. Mother Alexandra, the youngest daughter of Queen Marie of Romania.

———◆———

Q. What Washington native took over General MacArthur's command in the Philippines and was later the highest-ranking American POW in the Pacific Theater?

A. General Jonathan ("Skinny") Wainwright.

———◆———

Q. When was the Washington Cooperative Extension Program founded?

A. 1914.

———◆———

Q. What U.S. president served at Fort Vancouver for one year as a brevet captain?

A. Ulysses S. Grant.

———◆———

Q. What was the Columbus Day Storm?

A. The tail-end of Typhoon Freda hitting the Puget Sound.

———◆———

Q. What is the state motto?

A. *Alki* ("by and by" in Chinook).

———◆———

Q. Who is generally considered the father of Seattle?

A. Arthur A. Denny.

Q. What former president of the International Teamsters Union, who was sent to McNeil Island Penitentiary after facing racketeering charges, was granted a full pardon in 1975?

A. Dave Beck.

———◆———

Q. Who was Washington's first territorial governor?

A. Isaac Stevens.

———◆———

Q. When was the greatest snowstorm in Seattle's recorded history?

A. January 5–9, 1880, when six feet of snow fell.

———◆———

Q. What company, started in Washington in 1916, is the largest airplane manufacturer in the world?

A. Boeing.

———◆———

Q. How were bad cooks fired at logging camps?

A. A couple of hotcakes were nailed to the cook's door.

———◆———

Q. How many white Christmases have there been in Seattle?

A. Twelve since 1891.

———◆———

Q. When did Washington become a state?

A. November 11, 1889.

Q. What is the name of the John J. Astor trading vessel that was lost off Vancouver Island?

A. *Tonquin.*

◆

Q. In the mid-1960s, how many different versions of the Washington state seal were in use?

A. Over twenty-four.

◆

Q. Where did Harry Tracy, the infamous West Coast outlaw of the late 1800s, commit suicide?

A. Clinton.

◆

Q. To what organization can descendants of people who settled or were born in the Washington Territory belong?

A. Native Daughters of Territorial Pioneers of Washington.

◆

Q. In what church did Aimee Semple McPherson preach?

A. The First Congregational Church in Bellingham.

◆

Q. What year was the size of butter and margarine sticks deregulated in Washington?

A. 1988.

◆

Q. When were the three original reactors at the Hanford site completed?

A. 1945.

**Q.** What unusual financial event happened to Bill Gates, founder of Microsoft, in 1986?

**A.** He became a billionaire.

---◆---

**Q.** What class of Boeing plane dropped the atomic bombs on Nagasaki and Hiroshima?

**A.** B-29.

---◆---

**Q.** What missionary teacher, one of the first two white women to journey overland to the Northwest, worked as a team with her Presbyterian missionary doctor husband and was killed with him by Indians?

**A.** Narcissa Whitman, wife of Marcus Whitman.

---◆---

**Q.** What distinction does Northgate Mall in Seattle hold?

**A.** It is the world's first covered shopping mall.

---◆---

**Q.** The last stoplight on I-5 was removed in 1969 in what city?

**A.** Everett.

---◆---

**Q.** What was the first bed and breakfast in the state?

**A.** The James House in Port Townsend.

---◆---

**Q.** Where was the first prototype of a gas station set up in 1907?

**A.** The Seattle yard of the Standard Oil Company.

Q. What was the strongest recorded earthquake yet in state history?

A. 7.1 on April 13, 1949, in the Puget Sound.

---

Q. What long-time Washington director of highways was the project director for the Bay Area Rapid Transit (BART) system in San Francisco?

A. William A. Bugge.

---

Q. Where did Wapato John get the seeds for the first apple trees planted in North Central Washington?

A. From trees at Fort Vancouver.

---

Q. What company was the largest construction lime producer west of the Mississippi River until 1940?

A. The Roche Harbor Lime and Cement Company.

---

Q. At the junction of railroad and stagecoach lines along the Columbia River, schedules were deliberately made *not* to connect so passengers were forced to spend the night in what town, thus spending money there?

A. Coulee City.

---

Q. Who was the first white man to attempt to climb Mount Rainier?

A. William Fraser Tolmie (1833).

---

Q. Why did fish jump out of the Toutle River to die on land during the first Mount Saint Helens eruption?

A. The water was too hot.

Q. Who compiled the first dictionary of Chinook jargon?

A. Horatio Hale.

———————◆———————

Q. According to *Fortune* magazine, what company was rated the top exporting company in America in 1990 and 1991?

A. Boeing.

———————◆———————

Q. What business employs more people in the state than any other?

A. Farming.

———————◆———————

Q. How many casualties were there in the Pig War of 1859–1870?

A. One pig.

———————◆———————

Q. What Washington church at one time had the world's largest Presbyterian congregation?

A. Seattle's First Presbyterian Church (over 6,000 members).

———————◆———————

Q. What shop started the Nordstrom department store empire?

A. John W. Nordstrom's shoe store in Seattle.

———————◆———————

Q. What newspaperman, together with contractor Jim O'Sullivan, was responsible for convincing the state legislature to fund the Grand Coulee project?

A. Rufus Woods.

**Q.** What five-term lieutenant governor of Washington was a bandleader before he got into politics?

**A.** Vic Meyers.

◆

**Q.** Where and when was Washington's first gold strike?

**A.** Fort Colville in 1854.

◆

**Q.** According to the popular tall tale by George Estes, what were the original tracks of the Walla Walla & Columbia River Railroad made of?

**A.** Rawhide-covered wood rails.

◆

**Q.** Who was the first person of Chinese ancestry elected to public office in Washington?

**A.** Wing Luke (1960).

◆

**Q.** What function did the Puyallup fairgrounds once serve?

**A.** A Japanese internment camp (as Camp Harmony).

◆

**Q.** What distinction does the Clemons Tree Farm hold?

**A.** It is the first commercial tree-farm in the U.S.

◆

**Q.** What Spokane native became Speaker of the House?

**A.** Representative Tom Foley.

# ARTS & LITERATURE

## C H A P T E R   F O U R

Q. What Washington cartoonist has had his work displayed in the Smithsonian Institution?

A. Gary Larson.

———◆———

Q. What supermodel of the 1980s came from Leavenworth?

A. Laura Valentine.

———◆———

Q. Who popularized the Northwest style of architecure in the 1960s?

A. Paul Thiry, Ralph Anderson, and Pietro Belluschi.

———◆———

Q. Who are two of the best-known Palouse artists?

A. Robert Helm and Gaylen Hansen.

———◆———

Q. Vic Moore, Robert Helm, Gaylen Hansen, Jack Dollhausen, and Scott Fife have all had their work shown at what foreign gallery?

A. The Redmann Gallery in West Berlin.

**Q.** What museum's entire collection of Northwest Coastal Indian art has been photographed with the pictures made completely accessible by computer?

**A.** The Thomas Burke Memorial Washington State Museum.

———◆———

**Q.** What book by author Jim Faber is a collection of photographs of Northwest paddlewheel and sternwheel steamers?

**A.** *Steamer's Wake.*

———◆———

**Q.** International model Sasa Gudjonsson comes from what Seattle neighborhood?

**A.** Ballard.

———◆———

**Q.** Where is found the country's largest collection of Rodin sculptures acquired directly from the artist?

**A.** The Maryhill Museum.

———◆———

**Q.** What Seattle stained glass artisan has mastered the art of medieval glass painting?

**A.** Catherine Thompson.

———◆———

**Q.** Who carved the four new totem poles in Seattle's Pioneer Square?

**A.** Duane Pasco.

———◆———

**Q.** What book features Pat O'Hara's photographs of Washington?

**A.** *Washington Wilderness, the Unfinished Work.*

Q. What professional writing group originated the contest that collected the first stories for Joyce Delbridge's *Ferry Tales of the Puget Sound*?

A. Nightwriters of Vashon.

———◆———

Q. What Washington newspaper won a Pulitzer prize in 1981 for its coverage of the Mount Saint Helens eruption?

A. The Longview *Daily News*.

———◆———

Q. What Olympia school did *Harper's Bazaar* cover girl Michelle Streeter attend?

A. Capital High School.

———◆———

Q. What is the name of the auction that sells only the worst paintings?

A. The Point Roberts Auction.

———◆———

Q. To what does cartoonist Gary Larson attribute his success?

A. Caffeine.

———◆———

Q. What inspired Paul Horiuchi, considered by some the world master of contemporary collage, to make his first collage?

A. A bulletin board in Seattle's International District.

———◆———

Q. According to James Stevens, a writer who expanded on the tales of Paul Bunyan, what was the "true" origin of Puget Sound?

A. The unfinished grave of Babe the Blue Ox.

Q. What dessert, invented by Betsy Sestrap, has fifteen calories a spoonful and made the front page of the *New York Times*?

A. Fudge Sweet.

———◆———

Q. What folksinger from Spokane is known as the Great Voice of the Great Southwest?

A. Bruce ("Utah") Phillips.

———◆———

Q. What former Port Townsend resident wrote the best-selling novel *Dune*?

A. Frank Herbert.

———◆———

Q. Who wrote the novella *My Father, Combing My Hair*, which is based on her childhood at a U.S. Forest Service ranger station?

A. Brenda Peterson.

———◆———

Q. What IWW activist and songwriter was himself immortalized in song?

A. Joe Hill.

———◆———

Q. What famous designer did all the light fixtures in the Washington Capitol?

A. Louis B. Tiffany.

———◆———

Q. What is the name of the often well-dressed sculpture situated at the Fremont Bridge in Seattle?

A. *Waiting for the Interurban*.

**Q.** Why did Edward R. Murrow attend Washington State College at Pullman?

**A.** It offered the country's first course in broadcasting.

◆

**Q.** On the basis of what book did Angelo Pellegrini receive a Guggenheim Fellowship?

**A.** *The Unprejudiced Palate.*

◆

**Q.** What crime writer was once a detective in Seattle?

**A.** Dashiell Hammett.

◆

**Q.** What Washington artist was the first woman in the state to be licensed as a journeyman plumber?

**A.** Amy Burnett.

◆

**Q.** Even though Seaview residents Pat and Noel Thomas design and build houses in the $30,000–$40,000 price range, why is their work not advertised in the local real estate listings?

**A.** They design and build doll houses.

◆

**Q.** Where was illustrator and artist Jim Hays born?

**A.** On a Bothell cattle ranch.

◆

**Q.** Where did Pulitzer Prize-winning author Annie Dillard allegedly reside while she was writing *Holy the Firm*?

**A.** Lummi Island.

Q. What member of the Roosevelt family ran the Seattle *Post-Intelligencer* in the 1940s?

A. Anna Roosevelt Boettiger (with her husband, John).

---◆---

Q. What Seattle-based sculptor first made his way to the Northwest on a University of Washington athletic scholarship?

A. Tony Angell.

---◆---

Q. What is the tallest building west of the Rockies?

A. The seventy-six-story Columbia Center in Seattle (943 feet).

---◆---

Q. What did Seattle artist Richard Beyer originally title his public art project of a balding, potbellied bull sitting on a bench?

A. *Cowboy.*

---◆---

Q. If Paul Bunyan had been from Washington, what would he have been called instead of a lumberjack?

A. A logger.

---◆---

Q. Peter Simpson's book *City of Dreams* is about what city?

A. Port Townsend.

---◆---

Q. What Washington painter is regarded as the most important black artist in the United States?

A. Jacob Laurence.

**Q.** What popular American poet lived in Spokane's Hotel Davenport from 1924 to 1929?

**A.** Vachel Lindsay.

◆

**Q.** What Washington paper gave Mark Twain a bad review when he performed in its city?

**A.** *The Seattle Times.*

◆

**Q.** When was the first Governor's Writers Award given?

**A.** 1967.

◆

**Q.** What do Jimella Lucas, Evelyn Enslow, Diane Symms, Nanci Main, Terry De Blasio, Sandra Shea, and Kathy Casey have in common?

**A.** They are all respected chefs in the Northwest.

◆

**Q.** What Seattle-born-and-raised journalist, *Newsweek* columnist, and *Washington Post* editor won a Pulitzer Prize in 1978?

**A.** Meg Greenfield.

◆

**Q.** What Blaine native founded an internationally known school of arts?

**A.** Nellie C. Cornish.

◆

**Q.** What huge sculpture was built underneath the north end of the Aurora Bridge in Seattle?

**A.** A troll with a Volkswagen.

Q. What word did H. L. Mencken invent to describe Seattle-born burlesque queen Gypsy Rose Lee?

A. *Ecdysiast.*

———◆———

Q. What is special about the Pilchuck School?

A. It is the world's only school devoted to glassworking.

———◆———

Q. What Tacoma poet ended his life with a bullet in 1984?

A. Richard Brautigan.

———◆———

Q. *Ball Four* was Jim Bouton's best seller about his year with what Washington baseball team?

A. The Seattle Pilots.

———◆———

Q. Who invented the "happy face" symbol?

A. David Stern.

———◆———

Q. Who served as a Pasco city councilman and later headed the United Negro College Fund?

A. Arthur Fletcher.

———◆———

Q. Which Bremerton high school did L. Ron Hubbard, the founder of scientology, attend?

A. Union High School.

Q. What was western artist John Clymer's first sale?

A. A logo design for the Ellensburg Rodeo.

◆

Q. Who were the most famous characters created by one-time Puget Sound resident and author Elizabeth Montgomery?

A. Dick and Jane, of first-reader fame.

◆

Q. What 1928 novel by Bertrand Collins portrayed Seattle as the mythical town of Chinook?

A. *Rome Express.*

◆

Q. What novelist born in White Center was nominated for a Pulitzer Prize for *Death and the Good Life*?

A. Richard Hugo.

◆

Q. The Pacific Science Center in Seattle, the World Trade Towers in Manhattan, and the Century Plaza Towers in Los Angeles are all expressions of what Seattle-born architect's vision of "delight, serenity, and surprise"?

A. Minoru Yamasaki.

◆

Q. Gertrude Stein received a degree in what field when she graduated from the University of Washington?

A. Music.

◆

Q. What famous photographer opened a studio in Seattle in 1910?

A. Imogen Cunningham.

Q. What Okanogan-raised graduate of the University of Washington was portrayed by Robert Conrad in a television series based on his memoirs *Baa, Baa, Black Sheep*?

A. Gregory ("Pappy") Boyington.

◆

Q. E. B. White, the author of *Stuart Little* and *Charlotte's Web* among other books, was a reporter for which Washington paper?

A. *The Seattle Times*.

◆

Q. What fifth-generation carousel maker lives in Port Townsend?

A. William H. Dentzell III.

◆

Q. What modern dance leader was a faculty member at the Cornish College of the Arts?

A. Martha Graham.

◆

Q. What is the only magazine in the country devoted to coffee?

A. *Cafe Olé* (published in Seattle).

◆

Q. A pair of Chinese shoes from the Ch'ing dynasty was the inspiration for what well-known Seattle museum?

A. The Wing Luke Museum.

◆

Q. Who created the famous Fremont artwork *Waiting for the Interurban*?

A. Richard Beyer.

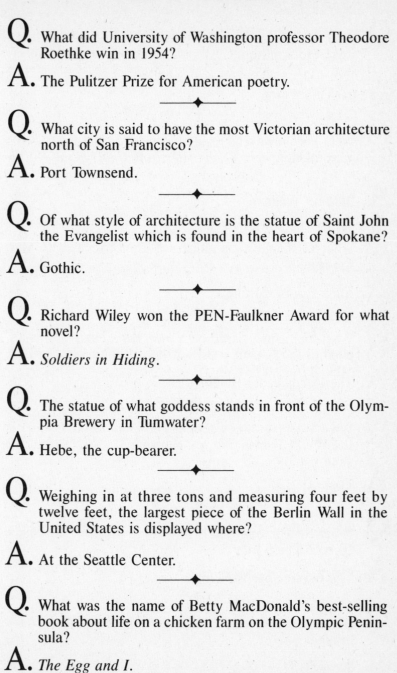

**Q.** What did University of Washington professor Theodore Roethke win in 1954?

**A.** The Pulitzer Prize for American poetry.

---

**Q.** What city is said to have the most Victorian architecture north of San Francisco?

**A.** Port Townsend.

---

**Q.** Of what style of architecture is the statue of Saint John the Evangelist which is found in the heart of Spokane?

**A.** Gothic.

---

**Q.** Richard Wiley won the PEN-Faulkner Award for what novel?

**A.** *Soldiers in Hiding.*

---

**Q.** The statue of what goddess stands in front of the Olympia Brewery in Tumwater?

**A.** Hebe, the cup-bearer.

---

**Q.** Weighing in at three tons and measuring four feet by twelve feet, the largest piece of the Berlin Wall in the United States is displayed where?

**A.** At the Seattle Center.

---

**Q.** What was the name of Betty MacDonald's best-selling book about life on a chicken farm on the Olympic Peninsula?

**A.** *The Egg and I.*

Q. Who designed most of the mansions in Spokane, then moved to Southern California and continued his profession?

A. Kirtland Cutter.

◆

Q. What Port Townsend resident designed Clint Eastwood's mayoral campaign T-shirt and wrote *Chefs of the Northwest*?

A. Barbara Williams.

◆

Q. What Washington journalist was good friends with Mao Tse-tung?

A. Anna Louise Strong.

◆

Q. What nickname, based on a *Star Wars* character, is applied to the Fourth and Blanchard Building in Seattle?

A. The Darth Vader Building.

◆

Q. What Washington resident has his print *Eagle Dancer* in the White House and his painting *The Veteran* in the state capitol in Olympia?

A. Michael Gentry.

◆

Q. What Seattle highrise is known as the Box the Space Needle Came In?

A. The old Seafirst Building.

◆

Q. Where is the national edition of the *New York Times* printed?

A. Tacoma.

Q. What structure has been called by the following nicknames: Umbrella, Orange Juice Squeezer, Big Mushroom, Condom, Giant Flywheel, Upside-Down Saucer,
and Flying Saucer?

A. The Kingdome.

◆

Q. What book did Seattle-born author Mary McCarthy
write?

A. *The Group.*

◆

Q. Approximately how many books are in the University of
Washington libraries?

A. 4.5 million.

◆

Q. Who won a Pulitzer Prize for his three-volume work
*Main Currents in American Thought*?

A. Vernon Louis Parrington.

◆

Q. What is the name of Dudley Carver's statue of a woman
incised into the side of a giant cedar outside Verlot at the
entrance to a never-completed park?

A. *Maiden of the Wood.*

◆

Q. What job did novelist Thomas Pynchon hold with the
Boeing Company from 1960 until 1962?

A. Technical writer.

◆

Q. What was the name of the Georgia artist who caused an
art world controversy with his composition *Seattle
Bible, 1989*?

A. Bill Paul.

Q. What University of Washington professor of English wrote the 1990 National Book Award winner *Middle Passage*, a novel about Rutherford Calhoun, a black cook aboard a slave ship?

A. Charles Johnson.

———◆———

Q. Who received the University of Washington's first diploma?

A. Clara McCarty (1876).

———◆———

Q. What overlooks the Columbia Gorge as a monument to Klickitat County's World War I dead?

A. A replica of Stonehenge.

———◆———

Q. Where is the largest collection of rosaries in the world?

A. Skamania County Historical Museum.

———◆———

Q. What weekly newspaper did Terry and Berta Pettus publish for the Washington Commonwealth Federation?

A. *The Washington New Leader.*

———◆———

Q. The Arctic Building in Seattle, built in 1916, is lined around the top with twenty-five of what creatures?

A. Walruses.

———◆———

Q. What is the name of the oldest weekly newspaper in Washington?

A. *Puget Sound Mail.*

Q. What two prestigious colleges has University of Washington graduate Virginia Smith headed?

A. Mills and Vassar.

———◆———

Q. What northwest magazine was bought by New Jersey Company Micromedia?

A. *Pacific Northwest.*

———◆———

Q. Why did the Yakima Indian Reservation appear in the pages of the *National Enquirer* in 1986?

A. Frequent UFO sightings.

———◆———

Q. What is special about the escalator in the Pioneer Square tunnel station of the Metro Bus Tunnel?

A. It is the longest and steepest escalator west of the Mississippi River.

———◆———

Q. To whom is inscribed the working model of Rodin's *Thinker,* which is at the Maryhill Museum?

A. Loie Fuller.

———◆———

Q. What Seattle native, sent to Japan for a formal Japanese education in 1959, revolutionized the design of fountains?

A. George Tsutakawa.

———◆———

Q. The nicknames Fairview Fanny and The Pig-I refer to what?

A. The *Seattle Times* and the Seattle *Post-Intelligencer,* daily newspapers in Seattle.

Q. The now-defunct *Cook's Magazine* named which Washington beverage as one of the nation's top four microbrews?

A. Redhook Extra Special Bitter.

◆

Q. What is the nickname for Washington State University?

A. Wazoo.

◆

Q. Bainbridge Island author Barbara Berger writes what kind of books?

A. Children's books.

◆

Q. What Northwest artist's designs won the 1948 competition for murals for the capitol in Olympia?

A. Kenneth Callahan.

◆

Q. Where is the oldest library in Washington?

A. The State Library in Olympia (founded in 1853).

◆

Q. What Washington writer won both the Hugo and Nebula awards for her science-fiction novel *Dreamsnake*?

A. Vonda N. McIntyre.

◆

Q. What Washingtonian draws the syndicated cartoon strip *The Far Side*?

A. Gary Larson.

**Q.** What Seattle artist drew *Dennis the Menace*?

**A.** Hank Ketcham.

---◆---

**Q.** What was the first book written by a resident of the Washington Territory?

**A.** *The Northwest Coast* by James G. Swain (1857).

---◆---

**Q.** Which newspaper, together with the Chicago *Tribune*, did Harry Truman identify as "the two worst newspapers in America"?

**A.** Spokane's *Spokesman Review*.

---◆---

**Q.** Who wrote the only Latin-Salish Indian dictionary?

**A.** Rev. Gregory Mengarini.

---◆---

**Q.** Which Washington town did Tom Robbins use for the setting of his novel *Another Roadside Attraction*?

**A.** Humptulips.

---◆---

**Q.** Who reported, "The nicest winter I ever spent was a summer in Seattle"?

**A.** Mark Twain.

---◆---

**Q.** Who described the University of Washington as "the university of a thousand years"?

**A.** Henry Suzzallo.

**Q.** What book by Ernest Callenbach described Washington's secession from the Union (together with Northern California and Oregon) to form a modern utopian state?

**A.** *Ecotopia.*

———◆———

**Q.** Author Betty MacDonald wrote a series of children's books featuring what character who lived on a small farm?

**A.** Mrs. Piggle-Wiggle.

———◆———

**Q.** Where was Owen Wister living when he wrote the novel *The Virginian* in 1902?

**A.** In the Okanogan.

———◆———

**Q.** What British poet said about Tacoma, "They are all mad here, all mad"?

**A.** Rudyard Kipling.

———◆———

**Q.** Which campus houses the largest collection of Indian art and artifacts in the Northwest?

**A.** Gonzaga University's Museum of Native American Cultures.

———◆———

**Q.** Where is the world's tallest single-strand totem pole?

**A.** Kalama.

———◆———

**Q.** Before becoming a writer of best-selling fantasy-adventure novels such as *The Sword of Shannara*, what was Washington author Terry Brooks' profession?

**A.** Lawyer (for seventeen years).

**Q.** What was the real name of the character Greta Pendrick, the thinly disguised heroine of *Rome Express*?

**A.** Guendolen Carkeek Plestscheeff.

---

**Q.** What novel by Washougal native Pamela Jekel begins with a mastodon hunt?

**A.** *Columbia*.

---

**Q.** What Oysterville author wrote *Words to Rhyme With*?

**A.** Willard Espy.

---

**Q.** What book was written by Michael Lawson and Gene Openshaw?

**A.** *Seattle Joke Book*.

---

**Q.** Washington State University at Pullman published "The Pronunciation Guide for Names in Washington State" to assist what group of people?

**A.** Broadcast announcers.

---

**Q.** The 1.3-mile Seattle Metro Bus Tunnel contains twenty-eight elevators, forty-six escalators, thirteen charted exits, and how many bathrooms?

**A.** None.

---

**Q.** For twenty years, why was it pointless to push the third-floor button in the elevator in the Mortvedt Library at Pacific Lutheran University?

**A.** There was no third floor.

Q. What Hugo and Nebula award-winning Washington author is best known for destroying or transforming the Earth in at least three of his novels?

A. Greg Bear.

———◆———

Q. What Washington state college has had student life there described as "experimenting their way to a diploma"?

A. Evergreen State College.

———◆———

Q. Who wrote *Walking the Beach to Bellingham*?

A. Harvey Manning.

———◆———

Q. Which of Raymond Chandler's short stories is set in Westport?

A. "Goldfish."

———◆———

Q. What is the name of the renowned Northwest garden writer?

A. Ann Lovejoy.

———◆———

Q. What book of Bob Pyle's featured the Willapa hills?

A. *Wintergreen*.

———◆———

Q. What University of Washington alumnus and Washington resident won the Governor's Writing Award for his novel *Shadow of Lies*?

A. Donald E. McQuinn.

**Q.** Poet Theodore Roethke lived in Edmonds for a time in the house of what artist friend?

**A.** Morris Graves.

———◆———

**Q.** Peter Max designed a postage stamp to commemorate what Washington event?

**A.** The World's Fair in Spokane.

———◆———

**Q.** Ezra Meeker, the founder of Puyallup, wrote what book?

**A.** *Pioneer Reminiscences of Puget Sound.*

———◆———

**Q.** What was the setting of Jayn Ann Krentz's first romance novel, *Gentle Pirates*?

**A.** Richland.

———◆———

**Q.** For what book did Washington author Audrey Wurdemann win the 1935 Pulitzer Prize in poetry?

**A.** *Bright Ambush.*

———◆———

**Q.** What Washington resident draws DC's *Green Arrow* comic books?

**A.** Mike Grell.

———◆———

**Q.** The threat of the sale and removal of a large sculpture in downtown Seattle by what famous sculptor sparked a months-long public furor?

**A.** Henry Moore.

**Q.** What is the translation of Evergreen State College's motto, *Omnia ex tares*?

**A.** Loosely, it means "let it all hang out."

———◆———

**Q.** What artist accompanied territorial governor Isaac Stevens to the Washington Territory?

**A.** Gustave Sohon.

———◆———

**Q.** From what county is playwright Janet Thomas?

**A.** Kitsap.

———◆———

**Q.** Who designed the Goodwill Arts Festival posters?

**A.** Ellen Ziegler.

———◆———

**Q.** What Japanese festival celebrated in Seattle does poet N. Bentley describe in the book *Sea Lion Caves*?

**A.** Bon Odori.

———◆———

**Q.** What famous writer had a job as a fire watcher at Desolation Peak in 1956?

**A.** Jack Kerouac.

———◆———

**Q.** In what profession has Charles Espy won every major award since 1978?

**A.** Bowmaker for musical instruments.

**Q.** Who painted the Fratelli's Ice Cream warehouse Holstein mural?

**A.** Chip Morse.

———◆———

**Q.** What Washingtonian wrote *All I Need to Know I Learned in Kindergarten?*

**A.** Robert Fulghum.

———◆———

**Q.** During the Pig War, 2nd Lt. Henry M. Roberts was stationed at Griffin Bay and later wrote what book?

**A.** *Roberts' Rules of Order.*

———◆———

**Q.** What former editor of *The Rocket* recently published a book entitled *Horse Latitudes?*

**A.** Robert Ferrigno,

———◆———

**Q.** The romance writer Linda Walters is a pen name composed of the first names of what wife and husband writing team?

**A.** Linda and Walter Rice.

———◆———

**Q.** Jayne Castle and Stephanie James are pen names of what internationally known romance novelist?

**A.** Jayne Ann Krentz.

———◆———

**Q.** Seattle writer Joanna Russ is famous for what groundbreaking novel?

**A.** *The Female Man.*

Q. What is the name of the writers' colony for women founded by Nancy Nordhof on Whidbey Island?

A. Hedgebrook Farm.

---

Q. What Washington university offers a year-round course on storytelling?

A. Eastern Washington University.

---

Q. Aside from being the editor of *The Rocket*, what other fan magazine does Charlie Cross edit?

A. *Backstreets* (a Springsteen fanzine).

---

Q. What publishing house printed a small (one thousand copies) edition of Jerry Gold's *Oedipus Cadet*?

A. Blackthorn Press.

---

Q. What is architect Sam Hill's most famous monument?

A. The Peace Arch at Blaine.

---

Q. What type of underground Northwest literature is characterized by circulating photocopies?

A. Northwest Samizdat.

---

Q. Dave and Judy Harrison are the owners of what Kirkland-based national magazine?

A. *Canoe*.

**Q.** What art activist saved the cherry tree in Pike Place Market's Post Alley from being cut down?

**A.** Buster Simpson.

◆

**Q.** What Orcas Island author wrote the children's book *Catalog* about mountains sending away for things from a mail-order catalog?

**A.** Jasper Tomkins.

◆

**Q.** What is the name of the modern retelling of the myth of Demeter and Persephone by Carol Orlock?

**A.** *The Goddess Letters.*

◆

**Q.** Whitman College was originally what kind of school?

**A.** A seminary.

◆

**Q.** What artist became famous painting scenes from the Pike Place Market and is possibly best known for his painting *Electric Night*?

**A.** Mark Tobey.

◆

**Q.** Nicholas O'Connell's book *At the Field's End* contains what type of literature?

**A.** Edited interviews with Northwest writers.

◆

**Q.** What is writer Ann Rule's literary genre?

**A.** Crime fiction.

Q. What scholar made recordings of Lushootseed story-tellers in the 1950s?

A. Leon Metcalf.

✦

Q. After writing a book about the United States, what London travel writer liked Washington so much he moved there?

A. John Raban.

✦

Q. Spokane's Audubon Story League, one of the largest storytelling guilds in the United States, is second only to what other guild?

A. The Seattle Storyteller's Guild.

✦

Q. The Rutter House in Spokane is thought to be the earliest example of what architectural style in the state?

A. Arts and Crafts style.

✦

Q. What book by Alan Cummings describes meandering through the San Juan Islands by boat?

A. *Gunkholing in the San Juans.*

✦

Q. Who gave Seattle the Seattle Art Museum?

A. Dr. Richard Fuller and his mother Margaret Fuller.

✦

Q. What Spokane native is best known for her unauthorized biographies of such public figures as Frank Sinatra and Nancy Reagan?

A. Kitty Kelley.

Q. In what Seattle hospital did author Thomas Wolfe stay in 1938?

A. Providence Hospital.

———◆———

Q. What does artisan Alan Zerobnick make?

A. Clown shoes.

———◆———

Q. In what art form does Seattle native Marsha Burns excel?

A. Photography.

———◆———

Q. Who donated the campus for Whitman College?

A. Dorsey Syng Baker.

———◆———

Q. What graduate school did humorist Patrick F. McManus attend?

A. Washington State University.

———◆———

Q. What title did Seattlite Lawrence Stone win?

A. Best Sommelier in the World.

———◆———

Q. Who was the first trained professional to be hired as the director of the Maryhill Museum?

A. Linda Brady Mountain.

**Q.** When was the Pantages Theater in Tacoma renovated?

**A.** 1983.

◆

**Q.** What Washington artist arranged over one hundred plaster and clay rabbits at the Seattle Art Museum to illustrate blind obedience in his piece titled *Rabbits*?

**A.** Jeffrey Mitchell.

◆

**Q.** *The Spotted Chicken Report,* put out by the Methow Valley Spotted Chicken Society, emphasizes what important kind of chicken information?

**A.** Chicken jokes.

◆

**Q.** How long did it take Anna Marie Collins to write the play *Angry Housewives*?

**A.** One and a half weeks.

◆

**Q.** What magazine was founded by a group of poets?

**A.** *Poetry Northwest.*

◆

**Q.** Sculptor Carlos Contreras' figure *Transformation,* in a private collection, depicts what activity?

**A.** A woman becoming a bird.

◆

**Q.** What Washington writer wrote about Ted Bundy in *Stranger Beside Me*?

**A.** Ann Rule.

**Q.** Huxley College is part of what university?

**A.** Western Washington University.

———◆———

**Q.** What paper was the first to write about damming the Columbia River at Grand Coulee Ravine?

**A.** *The Wenatchee World.*

———◆———

**Q.** What Evergreen State College alumnus and cartoonist wrote the play *The Good Times Are Killing Me*?

**A.** Lynda Barry.

———◆———

**Q.** The play *Suicide in B Flat*, which premiered in Seattle, was written by what famous actor/playwright?

**A.** Sam Shepard.

———◆———

**Q.** What is portrayed by *Ten Feet into the Future*, a sculpture by artist David Govedare?

**A.** Joggers.

———◆———

**Q.** What Tacoma-born printmaker, illustrator, and author of children's books won the 1939 Caldecott medal for his illustrations for *Mei Li*?

**A.** Thomas Handforth.

———◆———

**Q.** How old are the oldest known sculptures in the state (stone bowls in the shape of humans)?

**A.** Between 1,000 and 1,500 years old.

**Q.** How many buildings on the National Register of Historic Places were designed by Kirtland K. Cutter?

**A.** Over twenty.

---

**Q.** At what Seattle store can one choose from more than one million old, rare, and used books?

**A.** Shorey's Book Store.

---

**Q.** *Assault on Mount Helicon* is the autobiography of what Washington-born poet?

**A.** Mary Barnard.

---

**Q.** What Seattle restaurant won *Interior* magazine's national Restaurant Design award?

**A.** Casa U-Betcha.

---

**Q.** What Seattle literary group has a branch in Paris called *Les Invisibles*?

**A.** Invisible Seattle.

---

**Q.** What was the name of the father of landscape architecture who designed the Walla Walla park system, the state capitol grounds, and the University of Washington campus?

**A.** Frederick Law Olmstead.

---

**Q.** Winner of a National Endowment for the Arts grant, Ginny Ruffner works in what medium?

**A.** Glass.

# SPORTS & LEISURE

## CHAPTER FIVE

**Q.** With what is the Leavenworth Autumn Leaf Festival designed to coincide?

**A.** The Jonathan apple harvest.

◆

**Q.** Although the Puyallup Fair is one of the ten largest fairs in the United States, how does it differ from all other large fairs in Washington?

**A.** It is privately owned, not a state fair.

◆

**Q.** Yakima native Phil Mahre was the first American to win what championship in 1981?

**A.** The World Alpine Cup.

◆

**Q.** Who won a national contest for speed-stringing tennis rackets and has an outdoor and recreational equipment company named after him?

**A.** Eddie Bauer.

◆

**Q.** What Washington university relinquished the team name of "the Fighting Irish" in 1921?

**A.** Gonzaga.

Q. At the turn of the century, what sport did the Spokane Eagles play?

A. Baseball.

———◆———

Q. Who has won Omak's Suicide Race thirty-three out of forty-eight races, more than any other competitor?

A. Alex Dick.

———◆———

Q. Who are reputed to build the best hydroplanes in the world?

A. Ted Jones and his son, Ron Jones.

———◆———

Q. Where can one dine on Saturday night while watching the scenery between Ellensburg and Yakima?

A. Aboard the Spirit of Washington dinner train.

———◆———

Q. Frederich D. Huntress, the first teacher in Cowlitz County, is remembered for what unusual classroom behavior?

A. He would stop class to shoot ducks when he heard them fly overhead.

———◆———

Q. Who is one of the most famous baseball players in eastern Washington?

A. Steve Garvey.

———◆———

Q. What specific sport is the Great Canoe Race at Soap Lake?

A. Canoe relay racing.

Q. Harry Powers of Arlington was in what type of craft when he set the national altitude record of 22,750 feet?

A. An ultralight.

———◆———

Q. What is the name of the oldest fox hunting club west of the Mississippi River?

A. The Woodbrook Hunt Club.

———◆———

Q. Besides being considered the best downhill skiers in the United States, what else do Phil and Steve Mahre have in common?

A. They are twins.

———◆———

Q. Where is the Whisky Dick Triathlon held?

A. Ellensburg.

———◆———

Q. What championship golfer designed the eighteen-hole golf course at the Inn at Semiahmoo?

A. Arnold Palmer.

———◆———

Q. How many tourism regions does Washington have?

A. Seven.

———◆———

Q. During the rodeo months of July and August, how many rodeos are held in Washington, including pee wees and pros?

A. Fifteen.

Q. Where is the largest Fourth of July fireworks display west of the Mississippi?

A. Fort Vancouver.

———◆———

Q. Where was Washington's record steelhead (thirty-four pounds) caught?

A. On the East Fork of the Lewis River.

———◆———

Q. Dick Knight of Redmond participated in the longest three-set singles match in U.S. tennis history, a match that lasted for how long?

A. About five hours.

———◆———

Q. In 1978 the Seattle Smashers volleyball team briefly had what famous sports figure on its team?

A. Wilt Chamberlain.

———◆———

Q. What city was home to the Olympic boxing champions Sugar Ray Seales and Leo Randolph?

A. Tacoma.

———◆———

Q. Where in West Seattle is a manmade rock for practicing climbing?

A. Schurman Rock at Camp Long.

———◆———

Q. What former Minnesota Vikings assistant coach later became the first coach of the Seattle Seahawks?

A. Jack Patera.

**Q.** Who were the Seattle Pilots?

**A.** An American League baseball team in 1969.

———◆———

**Q.** Who were the participants in the only professional heavyweight boxing championship match ever held in Washington?

**A.** Floyd Patterson and Pete Rademacher (1957).

———◆———

**Q.** What is the nickname of the Cascades Alpine Guide, a three-volume set of books by Fred Beckey that identifies every mountain in the Cascades from the Columbia River to the Fraser River Valley?

**A.** Beckey's Bible.

———◆———

**Q.** "God made a few perfect heads, and to the rest, he gave hair" is the slogan for what contest at the Walla Walla Sweet Onion Festival?

**A.** The Bald-as-an-Onion contest.

———◆———

**Q.** Who was the manager of the Seattle Pilots in 1969?

**A.** Joe Shultz.

———◆———

**Q.** What was the name given to the storming of a Seattle football field by two thousand apple-throwing football fans from Wenatchee High School after losing a national event?

**A.** The Red Apple Riot of 1905.

———◆———

**Q.** What area is known as the golf capital of Washington?

**A.** The Tri-Cities.

**Q.** Doris Brown Heritage, winner of five consecutive cross-country championships, trained by running around what Seattle lake?

**A.** Greenlake.

———————◆———————

**Q.** What Washington volcano has the longest ski season?

**A.** Mount Baker.

———————◆———————

**Q.** What event features the Dinner Bell Handicap and wild-cow milking, occurs simultaneously with the Kittitas Fair, and is the largest event of its kind in the state?

**A.** The Ellensburg Rodeo.

———————◆———————

**Q.** From which city did George Frances Train, Washington's version of Phileas Fogg, begin his sixty-eight day trip around the world?

**A.** Tacoma.

———————◆———————

**Q.** In what event do the participants charge down a steep incline on horseback and ford a river that is sometimes so deep it washes the riders off?

**A.** The Omak Stampede and World-Famous Suicide Race.

———————◆———————

**Q.** What cities host the big-money rodeos in Washington?

**A.** Ellensburg, Omak, and Walla Walla.

———————◆———————

**Q.** What is the oldest ongoing festival in Washington?

**A.** Sequim's Irrigation Festival.

Q. Who was the first climber to die on Mount Rainier?

A. Prof. E. McClure, during his descent.

◆

Q. Where is one of the best places in Seattle to view Fourth of July fireworks?

A. The top of the Space Needle.

◆

Q. What rugby team is reputedly the best in Washington?

A. The Old Puget Sound Beach team.

◆

Q. What sport do the following teams play: the Spokane Chiefs, the Tri-City Americans, the Tacoma Rockets, and the Seattle Thunderbirds?

A. Ice hockey.

◆

Q. What is the greatest danger to people enjoying the outdoors in Washington?

A. Hypothermia.

◆

Q. What was the nickname of the original Miss Bardahl U-40 hydroplane, the National Unlimited champion and Gold Cup winner?

A. The Green Dragon.

◆

Q. What city holds a lilac festival each year?

A. Spokane.

Q. What was the name of the baseball team consisting of staff members of Washington state senators Dan Evans and Slade Gorton?

A. The Washington Senators.

———◆———

Q. What Seattle Seahawks linebacker left a ten-year, eleven-million-dollar contract to begin an acting career?

A. Brian ("the Boz") Bosworth.

———◆———

Q. What was the weight of the largest sturgeon hooked and later released in the Columbia River?

A. 1,200 pounds.

———◆———

Q. Who are the traditional rivals in Washington college football?

A. The Cougars and the Huskies.

———◆———

Q. From what Washington town did Yankees pitcher Mel Stottlemyre come?

A. Mabton.

———◆———

Q. Where and when is the world's largest free folk festival held?

A. The Northwest Folklife Festival at the Seattle Center on Memorial Day weekend.

———◆———

Q. Where can one bicycle through a section of old growth forest?

A. Tacoma's Point Defiance Park.

Q. What is considered a top prize in Washington beach-combing?

A. A Japanese glass fishing float.

———◆———

Q. Olympia is famous for what type of boat regatta?

A. Wooden boat.

———◆———

Q. What Bainbridge Island company has an international reputation for producing some of the best fly fishing rods in the world?

A. Sage.

———◆———

Q. What is a clam gun?

A. A two-foot-long metal tube with a crossbar handle at one end.

———◆———

Q. How many people have died trying to climb Mount Rainier?

A. Sixty-one (five less than have died in plane crashes in the park).

———◆———

Q. What narrow river, well known to whitewater rafting enthusiasts, plunges fifty feet per mile for fifteen miles?

A. Tilton.

———◆———

Q. Who leased the land for the Overlake Golf Club?

A. Norton Clapp.

**Q.** What is the rating in whitewater rafting of the Skykomish River?

**A.** Class IV "Boulder Drop."

---

**Q.** At what annual water race are the spectators expected to bomb the participants with water balloons?

**A.** Omak's Not-Quite-White-Water Race.

---

**Q.** What was the nickname of Seattle Supersonics basketball star Marvin Webster?

**A.** The Human Eraser.

---

**Q.** What was the nickname of Boone Kirkman, a nationally rated heavyweight boxer who hailed from Renton?

**A.** Boom Boom.

---

**Q.** What town has an annual feast that includes garlic in every dish?

**A.** Nahcotta.

---

**Q.** How many world's fairs have been held in Washington?

**A.** Three.

---

**Q.** What was the official name of the first world's fair held in Washington?

**A.** The Alaska–Yukon–Pacific Exposition.

Q. Where have Washington's World's Fairs been held?

A. Seattle (1909 and 1962) and Spokane (1974).

---

Q. What mountain was Hazard Stevens, the youngest Union general in the Civil War, determined to climb?

A. Mount Rainier.

---

Q. What lobbyist from Washington once played football at Notre Dame under Knute Rockne?

A. Francis ("Nordy") Hoffman.

---

Q. Which team—the Cougars or the Huskies—first played in the Rose Bowl?

A. The Cougars.

---

Q. Why would native Americans not climb Tahoma (Mount Rainier)?

A. It was considered sacred ground.

---

Q. Of the two fastest hydroplane tracks in the western United States, one is in San Diego, California, and the other is where?

A. Pasco.

---

Q. What was the name of the Seattle resident who was the winningest hydroplane driver in history?

A. Bill Muncey.

Q. What did John Wayne give to the people of Washington?

A. Twenty-three acres of land near Sequim Bay for a public marina.

———◆———

Q. Who did Wenatchee honor at early harvest festivals?

A. The Hesperides.

———◆———

Q. What are the names of Washington's two professional soccer teams?

A. Seattle Storm and Tacoma Stars.

———◆———

Q. What are the two intercollegiate sports to which the University of Washington charges no admission?

A. Women's and men's crew.

———◆———

Q. What baseball team founded in 1977 has consistently lost more games than it has won and is known as the "losingest franchise in major-league history"?

A. The Seattle Mariners.

———◆———

Q. What is the name of the oldest Thoroughbred racetrack on the West Coast?

A. Longacres, in Renton.

———◆———

Q. For whom are the Everett Giants baseball team the rookie league team?

A. The San Francisco Giants.

Q. What Washington hockey team won the 1991 Memorial Cup?

A. The Spokane Chiefs.

Q. What former member of the Seattle Thunderbirds went on to play with the Vancouver Canucks?

A. Petr Nedved.

Q. What do Juan Marichal, Gaylord Perry, Lyman Bostock, Willie McCovey, and Jose Canseco have in common?

A. They have all played for the Tacoma Tigers.

Q. What starts at Chief Timothy State Park, crosses the Snake River, and goes up the old Lewiston grade?

A. The thirteen-mile "I Made the Grade" Bicycle Ride.

Q. Orienteering, an exciting but obscure sport that requires running shoes and a compass, designates what Bothell resident as the number two woman orienteer?

A. Debbie Newell.

Q. When was the first year for the Port Angeles Salmon Derby?

A. 1937.

Q. The traditional rivalry between what two college football teams is worked out in the Apple Cup?

A. The Huskies and the Cougars.

Q. How did President John F. Kennedy officially open the 1962 World's Fair?

A. By remote control from Palm Beach, Florida.

———◆———

Q. What Washington man was the first American to climb to the summit of Mount Everest?

A. Jim Whittaker.

———◆———

Q. Former University of Washington student Li Jun Fan (Lee Yuen Kam) became nationally known by what name?

A. Bruce Lee.

———◆———

Q. What annual Seattle arts festival is named for an umbrella?

A. The Bumbershoot Festival.

———◆———

Q. What was the official name for the Seattle World's Fair of 1962?

A. The Century 21 Exposition.

———◆———

Q. How tall is the Space Needle?

A. 605 feet.

———◆———

Q. What are Liberty Cap, Point Success, and Columbia Crest?

A. Three peaks at the summit of Mount Rainier.

Q. In what year did a Washington football team first win the Rose Bowl?

A. 1916.

◆

Q. When and where is the Washington State Kite Festival?

A. Long Beach in August.

◆

Q. What is the most visited state park in Washington?

A. Deception Pass State Park.

◆

Q. What kind of rodeo takes place at the Washington State Apple Blossom Festival in Wenatchee?

A. Forklift.

◆

Q. "Do the Puyallup" refers to doing what?

A. Attending the annual Puyallup Fair.

◆

Q. What Olympic gold medalist from Washington, who at one time held every women's world record in swimming from 100 yards to one mile, was turned down for a job as a swimming instructor because she was a woman?

A. Helene Madison.

◆

Q. What is the oldest professional sport west of the Cascades?

A. Hydroplane racing.

Q. What horse won the Triple Crown in 1977?

A. Seattle Slew.

◆

Q. What national park was named a World Heritage site in 1981?

A. Olympic National Park.

◆

Q. Who was the oldest U.S. amateur champion of the British Open when he won it in 1904 at the age of forty-eight?

A. Jack Westland of Seattle.

◆

Q. What event takes place in Morton in August?

A. The Annual Logger's Jubilee.

◆

Q. Which city on the Puget Sound has an underwater park?

A. Edmonds.

◆

Q. Where does the annual hot-air balloon stampede begin?

A. Walla Walla.

◆

Q. In what part of the state is Potholes State Park?

A. Central Washington.

Q. What Washington governor coached the 1984 national champion girls' soccer team?

A. Booth Gardner.

◆

Q. Where was the record from the *Guinness Book of World Records* broken in 1990 for the largest sand sculpture ever built?

A. Long Beach.

◆

Q. In 1990 Washington hosted what major sports event created by Ted Turner?

A. The Goodwill Games.

◆

Q. What contribution to salmon fishing did Bill Boeing, Sr., make?

A. He invented the polar-bear hair fly.

◆

Q. Where is the Washington State Potato Conference and Trade Fair held?

A. Moses Lake.

◆

Q. In 1986 what Seattle Seahawk broke Harold Carmichael's record for consecutive regular-season games with at least one pass reception?

A. Steve Largent.

◆

Q. What tour, showcasing the Gorge, Diablo, and Ross hydroelectric power plants, started in 1928 as a one-time tour for thirty-five women of the Seattle Garden Club?

A. The Seattle City Lights Skagit Tour.

Q. When does the Puget Sound's Chilly Hilly Bicycle Ride take place?

A. February.

◆

Q. Where can one sign up for a cattle drive?

A. Early Winters Outfitters in Mazama.

◆

Q. What does the Gorge Report summarize for the Columbia Gorge?

A. Wind conditions for wind surfers.

◆

Q. What is the ratio of milk carton to weight used in Greenlake's annual Milk Carton Derby?

A. Twenty-five half-gallon milk cartons are required to support every one hundred pounds.

◆

Q. Ex-Seahawk Brian Bosworth referred to senior citizens by what term?

A. Blue hairs.

◆

Q. What Washingtonian who played third base for the St. Louis Browns had his picture on boxes of Wheaties?

A. Harlond B. Clift.

◆

Q. What national sports broadcaster announced for the University of Washington when Jim Owens was coach?

A. Keith Jackson.

**Q.** Where and when was the first baseball club in Washington formed?

**A.** Walla Walla, in 1866.

---◆---

**Q.** In what sport is a French handguard used?

**A.** Competitive oyster shucking.

---◆---

**Q.** What equipment is needed to enter a snodeo?

**A.** A snowmobile.

---◆---

**Q.** Where are Midwinter Outhouse Races held?

**A.** Conconully.

---◆---

**Q.** Who was the first woman to climb Mount Rainier?

**A.** Fay Fuller.

---◆---

**Q.** Why does the Bellevue Arts and Crafts Fair have a reputation for weather magic?

**A.** It has never rained on the fair.

---◆---

**Q.** Where are the world finals in drag racing held annually?

**A.** Raceway Park.

Q. How many horses have been killed in the Omak Stampede and World Famous Suicide Race in the last fifty-eight years?

A. Five.

———◆———

Q. Where is the West Coast Oyster Shucking Contest held each October?

A. At the Shelton Oysterfest.

———◆———

Q. Where can one take homegrown apples to be squeezed?

A. The Steilacoom Apple Squeeze.

———◆———

Q. Students from as far away as New Zealand, Norway, South America, and England have come to the Bar E Ranch outside Duvall to learn what skill?

A. Log cabin building.

———◆———

Q. How many clams did Joe Gagnon eat to set a world record?

A. 371.

———◆———

Q. Who is the highest paid sports figure in Washington?

A. Benoit Benjamin of the Seattle Supersonics.

———◆———

Q. What is the name of the Seafair Pirates' sailing vessel?

A. *Moby Duck.*

Q. What Washington event is known as one of the top ten air shows in North America?

A. The Washington International Air Fair in Everett.

———◆———

Q. Eddie Bauer brought sports star Olaf Ulland from Norway in 1940 to teach what new sport to Washingtonians?

A. Skiing.

———◆———

Q. When did the Washington State Cougars play in the Rose Bowl?

A. 1920, the bowl's second year.

———◆———

Q. How many times did the Pay'n'Pak team of Seattle win the Amateur Softball Association championship in the 1980s?

A. Five (1980, 1982, 1985, 1986, and 1987).

———◆———

Q. Where are the best places to fly a kite in Seattle?

A. Gasworks Park and Golden Gardens Park.

———◆———

Q. How many starting areas are there for Spokane's Lilac Bloomsday Run?

A. Three.

———◆———

Q. What is the rating for the Tacoma Tigers baseball team?

A. Triple-A.

Q. What island was once called Safari Island and stocked for sportsmen?

A. Spieden.

◆

Q. From the city of Gig Harbor, Dot held what world's record in 1937?

A. World's fastest racing rooster.

◆

Q. What sportscaster broadcasts the games of the Seattle Mariners?

A. Dave Niehaus.

◆

Q. What yacht club has hosted the Marine Daffodil Parade for over thirty years?

A. The Tacoma Yacht Club.

◆

Q. Where is the polo capital of the Pacific Northwest?

A. Spokane.

◆

Q. What sport requires warm clothes, an ice auger, tent heater, and a rod and tackle?

A. Ice fishing.

◆

Q. What game did Will Rogers play in Lake City a few days before his death?

A. Polo.

**Q.** How much does a Tyee Center membership at Husky Stadium cost?

**A.** $50,000.

———◆———

**Q.** Who were the Seattle Supersonics playing when a roof leak in the Coliseum caused the game to be stopped in January 1986?

**A.** The Phoenix Suns.

———◆———

**Q.** What Bremerton dentist carried a watermelon to the top of Mount Rainier?

**A.** Dr. Larry Heggerness.

———◆———

**Q.** Because of Phil and Steve Mahre, what area has become Washington's best-known ski area?

**A.** White Pass.

———◆———

**Q.** Prompted by a "sixth sense" feeling, what Washingtonian stopped climbing a day before reaching the top of Mount Everest?

**A.** Jim Wickwire.

———◆———

**Q.** What trip into the Middle Ages takes place outside of Carnation each year?

**A.** Camlann Medieval Faire.

———◆———

**Q.** Who was the king of "The King and His Court" softball touring team?

**A.** Eddy Feigner (who began in eastern Washington).

Q. What was the name of Western Washington University's experimental car that set a world's record for transcontinental fuel economy in the 1985 Unocal 76 Three Flags Econorally?

A. Viking 4.

———————◆———————

Q. What city hosted the first women's Olympic marathon trials in 1984?

A. Olympia.

———————◆———————

Q. What is the main sports attraction for the annual SeaFair Celebration?

A. The Rainier Cup Hydroplane Race.

———————◆———————

Q. How many annual festivals does Everett host each year?

A. Twenty-two.

———————◆———————

Q. The team named Martha's Moms competes in what sport?

A. Rowing.

———————◆———————

Q. Who is the legendary teacher of the Yakimas who serves as a guide at the dioramas at the Yakima Nation Cultural Center?

A. Spilyay.

———————◆———————

Q. Bernie Bickerstaff is head coach of what NBA team?

A. The Seattle Supersonics.

**Q.** Ocean Shores was once home to what annual golf classic?

**A.** The Pat Boone Celebrity Golf Classic.

———◆———

**Q.** Where is the annual Basset Wiener Race held on April Fool's Day?

**A.** Woodinville.

———◆———

**Q.** Who sponsors the Snowshoe Softball Tourney in Winthrop?

**A.** Three-fingered Jack's Saloon.

———◆———

**Q.** What street in Edmonds is named for a 1984 Olympic silver-medalist skater?

**A.** Rosalynn Sumners Boulevard.

———◆———

**Q.** The annual Mad Jack Masters Race features what type of skiing?

**A.** Giant slalom.

———◆———

**Q.** What local sport drew crowds of nearly one-half million in the 1950s?

**A.** Hydroplane racing.

———◆———

**Q.** Who were the first women to walk from Spokane to New York?

**A.** Helga and Clare Estby (1896).

Q. How many motorcycle clubs are there in Washington?

A. Over thirty.

———◆———

Q. The girls' and boys' cross-country teams from what Washington high school won the state championship in 1983 and 1987?

A. Edmonds High School.

———◆———

Q. What is the only requirement for membership in the Bureaucratic Bikers Motorcycle Club?

A. You must be a government employee.

———◆———

Q. How many stock car titles did Spokane native Edsol Sneva win before he quit?

A. Six.

———◆———

Q. The Flying Fiji Frogmen of what University of Washington fraternity leapfrogged from Seattle to Vancouver, British Columbia?

A. Phi Gamma Delta.

———◆———

Q. What is the name of the race track used at the Elma Slug Festival?

A. Shortacres.

———◆———

Q. After leaving the University of Washington Huskies, Joe Kelly went to what NFL team?

A. The Cincinnati Bengals.

Q. At what state university was was John Chaplin the track and field coach for over twenty years?

A. Washington State University.

———◆———

Q. Washington athlete Debbie Armstrong won Olympic gold in 1984 in what event?

A. Giant slalom.

———◆———

Q. Where and when was the first golf tournament held in the greater Seattle area?

A. At the country club on Bainbridge Island in 1896.

———◆———

Q. Where can one sleuth and grill the inhabitants of an entire town in pursuit of "who done it"?

A. Langley's Mystery Weekend.

———◆———

Q. What did early Washington state fans use as noise-makers to root for their teams?

A. Megaphones and cowbells.

———◆———

Q. In 1900, when the Huskies and the Cougars played against each other for the first time in football, who won?

A. Neither; it was a 5–5 tie.

———◆———

Q. Downhill skiing is the usual sport at Snoqualmie Pass, but what sport are more people stepping into?

A. Snowshoeing.

Q. What is the name of the second-largest regional kite flying club in the country?

A. The Washington State Kite Fliers Association.

◆

Q. What novel sports event did the 1909 World's Fair sponsor?

A. An auto race from New York to Seattle.

◆

Q. The Sonics traded Jack Sikma to what team?

A. The Milwaukee Bucs.

◆

Q. What day each year do the Z Canyon Square Dancers dance atop Boundary Dam's turbines?

A. Mother's Day.

◆

Q. What is the featured event of the White Pass Winter Carnival?

A. Snow sculpting.

◆

Q. Spokane closes its streets for two weeks each summer for what sporting event?

A. The Washington Trust Cycling Classic.

◆

Q. Where do the vintage motorcyclists go for their annual road rally?

A. Vashon Island.

Q. Since they have no professional football team of their own, fans from what state regularly charter planes to attend Seahawks games?

A. Alaska.

------◆------

Q. X-Man is the monicker of what Seattle Supersonic?

A. Xavier McDaniel.

------◆------

Q. Where did figure skater Scott Williams train in Tacoma?

A. Sprinker Recreation Center.

------◆------

Q. Sports fisherman Tom Peterman pulled the state record catfish, weighing 32½ pounds, from what lake?

A. Lake Aspen.

------◆------

Q. Spokane resident Elizabeth Klobusicky-Marlaender was a member of the first American team to successfully climb what?

A. Annapurna (in the Himalayas).

------◆------

Q. What important position does Sundodger Denali have with the University of Washington Huskies?

A. Mascot.

------◆------

Q. What is the name of the first black woman professional race car driver?

A. Cheryl Linn Glass (from Seattle).

Q. Where were the team trials for the 1936 Winter Olympics held?

A. Paradise.

———◆———

Q. What Grand Prix race set the current standard for all street-style races in the world?

A. The 1986 Schuck's Grand Prix Tacoma.

———◆———

Q. What Seattle native coined the term *windsurfing*?
A. Bert Salisbury.

———◆———

Q. What Denver Broncos quarterback was born in Washington?

A. John Elway.

———◆———

Q. Where can one enjoy a "howl-in" with real wolves?
A. Wolf Haven in Tenino.

———◆———

Q. The Richland High School Bombers use what image as their logo?

A. A mushroom cloud.

———◆———

Q. What is the first county fair of the season in the state of Washington?

A. The Asotin County Fair and Rodeo.

# SCIENCE & NATURE

## CHAPTER SIX

Q. What profession do Washingtonians Bonnie Dunbar, Steven S. Oswald, Richard F. Gordon, and Francis Scobee have in common?

A. Astronaut.

◆

Q. Where and when was the last reported case of bubonic plague in Washington?

A. Tacoma in 1921.

◆

Q. What is the largest amount ever paid for a tree?

A. $51,000 for a Starkspur Golden Delicious apple tree in Yakima.

◆

Q. What are the symmetrical four-to-six-foot-high bumps found on several miles of prairie in Thurston County?

A. Mima Mounds.

◆

Q. What University of Washington graduate and audio equipment manufacturer was called by *Audio* magazine "the latest acknowledged guru of the audio world?"

A. Bob Carver.

Q. What is another name for Bigfoot?

A. Sasquatch.

◆

Q. Where is a collection of Pratt & Whitney engines from the 1920s?

A. Boeing's Museum of Flight.

◆

Q. In what area are most of Washington's 5.3 million egg-laying hens?

A. Within one hundred miles of Seattle.

◆

Q. Who gave Yakima a pair of Brill electric trolleys?

A. The city of Porto, Portugal.

◆

Q. A Washington State University professor believes Sasquatch is a descendant of what ancient primate?

A. *Gigantopithecus.*

◆

Q. What astronaut from Washington died in the Challenger Shuttle explosion?

A. Francis Scobee.

◆

Q. What priest of the Wanapun tribe announced he had risen from Mother Earth, then told his followers to return to the old ways in the face of the white man's encroaching religion?

A. Smohalla.

Q. What is a green and white double-ender?

A. A Washington state ferry.

---◆---

Q. When Camp Grisdale, near Shelton, closed in 1986, what distinction did it hold?

A. It was the last residential logging camp in the lower forty-eight states.

---◆---

Q. Where is a collection of fire helmets from as far away as Havana and Australia?

A. In the Hall of Fire Engines at the Washington State Fire Service Historical Museum.

---◆---

Q. What is the Washington state rock?

A. Petrified wood.

---◆---

Q. Who were the world's tallest cowboys?

A. Ben Hutcheson (6′8″) and his brother Sam (7′4″) (from eastern Washington).

---◆---

Q. What Washington zoo went from the Humane Society's "worst ten" list to being lauded by the BBC series "Zoo 2000" as "unparalleled among big-name zoos"?

A. The Point Defiance Zoo.

---◆---

Q. What world-renowned Hutterite scholar lives near Reardan at the Espanola Colony?

A. Paul Gross.

**Q.** Why is the COMSAT station situated near the town of Brewster?

**A.** It is so sparsely settled that there is little electronic interference.

―――――◆―――――

**Q.** What Thurston County pioneer is thought to have brought the first dandelion seeds to the state for use in her healing potions?

**A.** Kitty Simmons Maynard.

―――――◆―――――

**Q.** What Seaview resident won acclaim as the "original native man" for his ability to go out into the wilderness naked and alone and survive?

**A.** Joe Knowles.

―――――◆―――――

**Q.** What enterprising Sumner woman worked her way through graduate school by delivering llama-grams?

**A.** Florence Dix.

―――――◆―――――

**Q.** What 1906 central Washington event involved 300 cowboys and 2,400 horses?

**A.** The last big roundup of wild horses in Washington.

―――――◆―――――

**Q.** What does a tin of Cougar Gold contain?

**A.** Washington State University-made cheese.

―――――◆―――――

**Q.** During the electrical dimout of 1949, what was brought to Tacoma to be hooked into its power grid to augment the system?

**A.** A battleship.

**Q.** According to the *Seattle Times*, what would Lake Union become filled with if the Aurora Bridge were built?

**A.** Wrecked cars.

◆

**Q.** What is the meaning of the Indian word *appaloosa*?

**A.** "Horse of the rolling hills."

◆

**Q.** Where was built the world's first totally underground electricity generating plant?

**A.** Snoqualmie Falls (1898).

◆

**Q.** What was the colloquial term for the itinerant workers who followed the apple harvest?

**A.** Apple knockers.

◆

**Q.** What apple has such a delicate skin that pickers have to use cotton gloves so as not to damage it?

**A.** The Stayman–Winesap.

◆

**Q.** Washington is the nation's second leading producer of what fruit?

**A.** Pears.

◆

**Q.** What is the name of the world's only streamlined ferry, produced at the Kirkland Shipyard?

**A.** *Kalakala.*

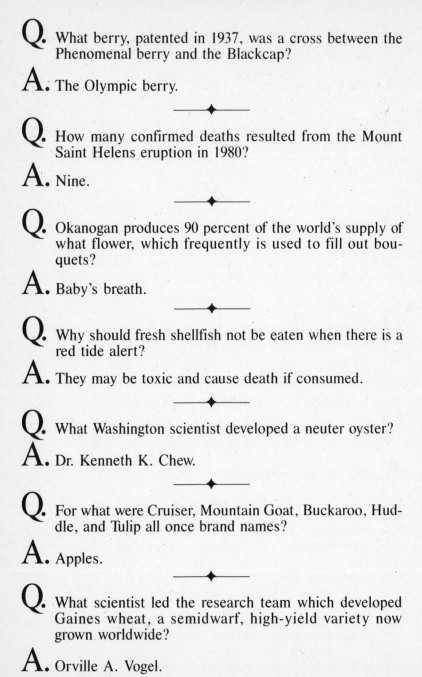

Q. What berry, patented in 1937, was a cross between the Phenomenal berry and the Blackcap?

A. The Olympic berry.

———◆———

Q. How many confirmed deaths resulted from the Mount Saint Helens eruption in 1980?

A. Nine.

———◆———

Q. Okanogan produces 90 percent of the world's supply of what flower, which frequently is used to fill out bouquets?

A. Baby's breath.

———◆———

Q. Why should fresh shellfish not be eaten when there is a red tide alert?

A. They may be toxic and cause death if consumed.

———◆———

Q. What Washington scientist developed a neuter oyster?

A. Dr. Kenneth K. Chew.

———◆———

Q. For what were Cruiser, Mountain Goat, Buckaroo, Huddle, and Tulip all once brand names?

A. Apples.

———◆———

Q. What scientist led the research team which developed Gaines wheat, a semidwarf, high-yield variety now grown worldwide?

A. Orville A. Vogel.

Q. Where can one pick a peck of peppers (sixty-three varieties) at the beginning of August?

A. The Krueger Pepper Gardens in Wapato.

◆

Q. Writer David Tirrell Hellyer created what wildlife sanctuary near Tacoma?

A. Northwest Trek.

◆

Q. What do the wine grapes Riesling, Chenin Blanc, Gewürztraminer, Semillion, Cabernet Sauvignon, Merlot, and Pinot Noir have in common?

A. They are the most successful wine grapes grown in Washington.

◆

Q. Most of the 25 million pounds of what product grown in the Palouse is shipped primarily to Egypt, Colombia, Italy, Spain, and Venezuela?

A. Lentils.

◆

Q. For ten cents, where can one get a marble exposed to gamma radiation?

A. At the Hanford Science Center.

◆

Q. What potato is considered the best in Washington?

A. The Yellow Finn.

◆

Q. What was reported to have surfaced in Lake Washington during the 1965 earthquake?

A. A Loch Ness-type creature.

Q. Compared to California's 50,000 acres, how many acres in Washington are suitable for vineyards?

A. 250,000 (only 30,000 are currently in production).

◆

Q. What was the length of the longest sturgeon yet found in lake Washington?

A. Eleven feet.

◆

Q. Why are Washington apples banned in Japan, China, and Korea?

A. Concern over coddling moth infestation.

◆

Q. What tireless promoter of Washington grapes holds the title Supreme Knight of the Brotherhood of the Knights of the Vine?

A. Walter Clore.

◆

Q. Where are the largest mule deer in the state found?

A. The Methow Valley.

◆

Q. What Northwest shipbuilder's designs have been used to build over 16,000 vessels?

A. H. C. Hanson.

◆

Q. Why was the city of Newcastle so named?

A. It was the major coal producing town in Washington (like the city in England).

Q. What is the most poisonous plant found in Washington?

A. Western water hemlock.

———◆———

Q. What information does one get by dialing 1-976-RAIN?

A. Weather forecasts around the state.

———◆———

Q. What is the number one farm export from Washington ports?

A. Wheat.

———◆———

Q. When were the first Pacific oysters planted in Willapa Bay?

A. 1928.

———◆———

Q. What is the Mystic Lake Dairy's particular claim to fame?

A. It is the largest goat milk dairy in Washington.

———◆———

Q. What percentage of oysters produced on the Pacific Coast come from Washington waters?

A. Ninety-six percent.

———◆———

Q. What is the world's smallest edible oyster?

A. The Olympia oyster (2" by 2").

Q. What insect stimulates mint oil production?

A. The orange mint moth.

---

Q. How much of the cheese consumed in Washington is imported from out of state?

A. Over seventy-five percent.

---

Q. What two pets are not restricted by Seattle leash laws?

A. Cats and pigeons.

---

Q. When were the first 70,000 cases of Rainier beer sent to Taiwan?

A. 1987.

---

Q. What subspecies of trout is named after an admiral of the U.S. Navy?

A. *Salmo gairdneri beardsleei* (Beardslee's trout).

---

Q. What former national director of the John Birch Society and Yakima resident is best known for inventing the small plastic square that keeps plastic bread bags closed?

A. Floyd Paxton.

---

Q. Walter Brattain, an alumnus of Whitman College and winner of the 1956 Nobel Prize for physics, is best known for what invention?

A. The transistor (he was co-inventor).

**Q.** What native son of Entiat, together with his colleague Dr. William Waugh, isolated vitamin C?

**A.** Charles Glen King.

———————◆———————

**Q.** What University of Washington professor of education improved upon the QWERTY typewriter keyboard?

**A.** August Dvorak.

———————◆———————

**Q.** What is the name of the tube invented by Belding Scribner that prevents vessel collapse in dialysis patients?

**A.** Scribner cannula.

———————◆———————

**Q.** Which elementary school was renamed for Dick Scobee?

**A.** North Auburn Elementary School.

———————◆———————

**Q.** Where was Marmes Man, the oldest human remains found in the New World, discovered?

**A.** Above the Palouse River in a rock shelter near Lyons Ferry.

———————◆———————

**Q.** What company was founded in 1916 under the name of Pacific Aero Products?

**A.** The Boeing Company.

———————◆———————

**Q.** What city has the largest number of doctors for its size in the United States?

**A.** Wenatchee.

Q. Where is the Aplets & Cotlets factory?

A. Downtown Cashmere.

◆

Q. What has been called "the most obscene looking clam in the world"?

A. The geoduck (pronounced "gooey-duck").

◆

Q. What stayed aloft for eight hours, fifty-two minutes, without power?

A. The *Yakima Clipper*, a fifty-foot sailplane.

◆

Q. What extraordinary plant did Lewis and Clark note that the native Americans used to weave virtually watertight baskets?

A. Beargrass.

◆

Q. What do the Hood Canal, the Evergreen Point, and the Mercer Island bridges have in common?

A. They are all floating bridges.

◆

Q. Why do peregrine falcons come to Seattle?

A. To dine on Seattle's pigeons.

◆

Q. What type of gemstone used in expensive jewelry is called Ellensburg Blue and is only found in the Ellensburg area?

A. Agate.

Q. What waterway is home to the world's largest species of octopus (up to twelve feet across and weighing thirty pounds)?

A. Puget Sound.

◆

Q. What are Ice Harbor, Lower Monumental, Little Goose, and Lower Granite?

A. Dams on the Snake River.

◆

Q. The arrival of Lewis and Clark at what location marked the end of the mission President Jefferson had assigned them?

A. Baker's Bay.

◆

Q. What did Emanual Manis find while digging a pond on his farm outside Sequim?

A. Two mastodon tusks.

◆

Q. What served as a navigation beacon on Scarborough Head, a bluff overlooking the Columbia River?

A. A large grove of fruit and hawthorn trees.

◆

Q. What onion is named after a town in Washington?

A. The Walla Walla Sweet.

◆

Q. Who was the "Johnny Appleseed of Wenatchee"?

A. Phillip Miller.

Q. Who built a full-sized replica of the Wright Brothers' 1902 glider?

A. Students at the University of Washington.

———◆———

Q. What Washington city is the iris, tulip, and narcissus capital of the world?

A. Mount Vernon.

———◆———

Q. Where do the Dutch come to buy their tulips?

A. The Skagit Valley.

———◆———

Q. What was the proudest childhood accomplishment of William O. Douglas, former U.S. Supreme Court justice?

A. Picking 400 pounds of cherries in one day.

———◆———

Q. What plant, commonly used as low-maintenance groundcover near highways, was brought to the Northwest by the Sisters of Notre Dame de Namur in the 1840s?

A. Scotch broom.

———◆———

Q. Sixty percent of Washington's income from minerals derives from the quarrying and production of what substances?

A. Cement, stone, and gravel.

———◆———

Q. What animal is the mascot of Evergreen State College?

A. The geoduck.

Q. What animals, which congregate along Everett Harbor's jetty from December through June, are known collectively as "the Everett Gang"?

A. California sea lions at the northern end of their migration.

———◆———

Q. What is the correct name for a landlocked sockeye salmon?

A. Kokanee.

———◆———

Q. What happened on May 18, 1980?

A. Mount Saint Helens erupted.

———◆———

Q. What is the driest month of the year in Washington?

A. July.

———◆———

Q. For what meteorological phenomena is Cape Disappointment noted?

A. It is the foggiest place on the West Coast.

———◆———

Q. Where is the Gallery of Electricity?

A. Rocky Reach Dam.

———◆———

Q. What is the specialty of the Conner Zoological Museum?

A. Western vertebrates.

Q. One hundred tons of what accumulation was picked up from Washington beaches on September 15, 1990?

A. Mostly plastic debris.

◆

Q. How many different native American languages do philologists estimate were spoken in Washington?

A. As many as forty.

◆

Q. What is the Washington state tree?

A. Western hemlock.

◆

Q. What native wood is used for smoking meats and barbecuing?

A. Alder.

◆

Q. Where does the world's largest surviving Sitka spruce (*Picea sitchensis*) stand?

A. Near Lake Quinalt.

◆

Q. An Aplet or a Cotlet is what kind of Washington confection?

A. A jellied fruit candy.

◆

Q. How many fish hatcheries are there in Washington?

A. Twenty-six.

**Q.** How many dams are on the Columbia River?

**A.** Fourteen.

---

**Q.** What does ASARCO stand for?

**A.** American Smelting and Refining Company.

---

**Q.** According to legend what is said to inhabit Mount Rainier?

**A.** A race of subterranean humans.

---

**Q.** What is the longest glacier in the continental United States?

**A.** The five-mile-long Emmon Glacier atop Mount Rainier.

---

**Q.** What are the three wettest months in Washington?

**A.** November, December, and January.

---

**Q.** What tree, originally mistaken for magnolia, is native to Seattle's Magnolia Bluff?

**A.** Madrona.

---

**Q.** What was the first huge dam on the Columbia River?

**A.** The Bonneville Dam.

Q. What species of crab was named for a Washington city?

A. Dungeness.

Q. What is the Washington state animal?

A. The Roosevelt elk.

Q. What county has averaged forty bushels of wheat per acre since 1934?

A. Whitman.

Q. What is the Washington state flower?

A. Western rhododendron.

Q. All the wheat from Whitman County is made into what food product?

A. Pasta.

Q. What Washington company is the largest manufacturer of lumber in the world?

A. Weyerhaeuser.

Q. What is the Tacoma Dome's claim to fame?

A. It is the world's largest wooden dome.

Q. What rare birds live in the Skagit fields?

A. Snow geese from Siberia and trumpeter swans.

◆

Q. What is the Washington state fish?

A. Steelhead trout.

◆

Q. How much dust, ash, and debris did Mount Saint Helens eject in the May 18, 1980, eruption?

A. About a cubic mile.

◆

Q. What is the tallest volcano in the lower forty-eight states?

A. Mount Rainier.

◆

Q. The Hecla Mines in Ferry County are the nation's second largest producer of what mineral?

A. Gold.

◆

Q. At 178 feet tall and 61 feet in diameter, where is the world's largest western red cedar?

A. Near Forks.

◆

Q. Where is the only known mastodon kill site in North America?

A. Near Sequim on the Olympic Peninsula.

Q. What Washington county is home to North America's smallest mammal, the pygmy shrew?

A. Pend Oreille.

◆

Q. What is the highest temperature recorded in Seattle?

A. 100 degrees.

◆

Q. Why is the Ozette Indian Village one of the most important archaeological sites in North America?

A. It was occupied continuously by the Makah Indians for four thousand years until the 1930s.

◆

Q. At 12,596 feet long, what is Washington's longest floating bridge?

A. The Evergreen Point Floating Bridge on Lake Washington.

◆

Q. Who produced the first evaporated milk?

A. The Carnation Company in Kent (in the 1890s).

◆

Q. What was the Okanogan's "earth cookie"?

A. An unexplained slab of earth (10′ x 8′ x 2′) cut from the ground and moved seventy feet away.

◆

Q. Where and when was the first hydroelectric plant west of the Mississippi built?

A. In Spokane Falls, in 1885.

Q. Who built the first electric street light system in the United States?

A. George A. Fitch.

———◆———

Q. What happens in the Skagit Valley every spring?

A. Over one thousand acres of tulips, daffodils, and irises bloom.

———◆———

Q. What do the Hood Canal, the Mercer Island, and the Tacoma Narrows bridges have in common?

A. They were all sunk by high winds.

———◆———

Q. Where is the world's longest log flume, a water trough on trestles, operated?

A. On a nine-mile stretch that ends in Underwood.

———◆———

Q. Where is Wolf Haven, the only private nonprofit wolf sanctuary in the United States?

A. Near Tenino.

———◆———

Q. Where did the seeds for reforesting Germany's Black Forest come from?

A. The North Cascades National Forest.

———◆———

Q. What is special about the Boeing Company's main assembly plant in Everett?

A. It has the largest interior cubic capacity in the world.

Q. What fruit is it illegal to bring into Washington?

A. Homegrown apples (because of apple maggots).

———◆———

Q. Who holds the dubious distinction of shooting the last gray wolf on Graywolf River?

A. A. J. Cameron.

———◆———

Q. What unique instrument is found at Goldendale Observatory State Park.

A. The country's largest public telescope.

———◆———

Q. How much height did Mount Saint Helens lose in the May, 1980 eruption?

A. 1,313 feet.

———◆———

Q. What was the Corps of Discovery?

A. The official name of the Lewis and Clark expedition.

———◆———

Q. What are the Makah, Queets, Quinalt, Skokomish, Squaxin Island, Suquamish, Klallam, and Quileute?

A. Some of the native American tribes on the Olympic Peninsula.

———◆———

Q. How many native American tribes lived east of the Cascades?

A. Sixteen.

**Q.** Where is the Gypsy Children's Program, the only public school for children of Gypsies?

**A.** Seattle.

---◆---

**Q.** From what Indian tribe is the word *appaloosa* derived?

**A.** The Palouse.

---◆---

**Q.** Where in the lower forty-eight states is found the largest concentration of bald eagles?

**A.** The San Juan Islands.

---◆---

**Q.** What state park was once the site of a prehistoric forest?

**A.** Ginkgo Petrified Forest State Park.

---◆---

**Q.** What is as high as a forty-six-story building, twelve city blocks long, and was, when it was completed in 1940, the world's largest concrete structure?

**A.** Grand Coulee Dam.

---◆---

**Q.** What is the name of the car made by the Henderson Motor Company of Bellingham?

**A.** Avion.

---◆---

**Q.** What does the acronym WPPSS (commonly pronounced "whoops") stand for?

**A.** Washington Public Power Supply System.

Q. What test pilot demonstrated the new Boeing 707 in 1955 by doing two slow barrel rolls at five hundred feet over the crowd on Seafair Sunday?

A. A. M. ("Tex") Johnston.

◆

Q. How much does the largest Ellensburg Blue agate ever found weigh?

A. Six pounds.

◆

Q. The country's largest collection of what commercial necessity of pioneer times does the Museum of Native American Cultures have?

A. North American trade beads.

◆

Q. For what is Bickleton famous?

A. It is the bluebird capital of America.

◆

Q. What is special about the Cascade Tunnel?

A. It is the longest railroad tunnel in the country.

◆

Q. What is the collective name given to the salmon-eating sea lions at the Chittenden Locks?

A. Herschel.

◆

Q. How many of the original five nuclear power plants that were part of the WPPSS project are still running?

A. One (at Hanford).

Q. Where is the oldest operating airfield in the United States?

A. The Pearson Airpark Museum in Vancouver.

———◆———

Q. Most of Washington's wine producing areas are on the same latitude as what European wine producing areas?

A. The Burgundy and Bordeaux provinces of France.

———◆———

Q. What is Chuckanut Mountain made of?

A. Fossilized sandstone.

———◆———

Q. What is a chinook?

A. A warm wind.

———◆———

Q. What plant, known as "young life maker," did native Americans use to make rugs, capes, baskets, and over one hundred other things?

A. Western red cedar.

———◆———

Q. At the current rate of logging, how many years are left before all the western red cedars are cut down?

A. Between twenty-five and forty years.

———◆———

Q. Who invented the first goose-down jacket?

A. Eddie Bauer.

Q. What were the glaciated peaks of the North Cascades 500 million years ago?

A. Ocean floor.

———◆———

Q. The average temperature for eastern Washington is how many degrees hotter than that of western Washington?

A. Ten degrees.

———◆———

Q. What is the Washington state bird?

A. Willow goldfinch.

———◆———

Q. Who are Sylvia and Sylvester?

A. Two mummies at Ye Olde Curiosity Shop on Seattle's Waterfront.

———◆———

Q. What requirement is necessary to observe while hunting the Ellensburg Blue agate?

A. Don't bother the cows.

———◆———

Q. What is the nickname for someone who has lived in Washington a long time?

A. A mossback or mossyback.

———◆———

Q. Who, in 1983, won the first John and Nora Lane Award for the most successful Bluebird Trail program?

A. Jess and Elva Brinkerhoff.

Q. Found in gardens, what are ochre ringlets, Mormon frit-illaries, checkered whites, Lorquina admirals, and West Coast painted ladies?

A. Butterflies.

◆

Q. What ex-Lakeside School student is considered America's youngest billionaire?

A. Bill Gates.

◆

Q. What former Boeing engineer developed the first take-apart kayak?

A. Peter Kaupat.

◆

Q. A device containing two seven-pound balls, a pendulum suspended in warm water, and a six-pound pillow strapped around the ribs with a tight belt to constrict the lungs was invented by Linda Ware for what purpose?

A. Called "the empathy belly," it mimics the feeling of pregnancy.

◆

Q. What town boasted the largest lumbermill in the world at the turn of the century?

A. Cosmopolis.

◆

Q. What is the reputed source for the bacterial pollution in Quilcene Bay?

A. Diarrhetic harbor seals.

◆

Q. What Washington State University scientist was named to the prestigious National Academy of Sciences?

A. Bud Ryan.

Q. What newly discovered species of chewing louse found only in owls is named after a Washington cartoonist?

A. *Strigiphilus garylarsoni.*

◆

Q. What shipyard built replicas of the *Lady Washington*, the first American ship to sail to Japan, and the *Columbia Rediviva*, the first American ship to sail around the world?

A. The Grays Harbor Shipyard.

◆

Q. Washington geneticists Andy Kleinhofs and Steve Knapp are making a genetic map of what plant?

A. Barley.

◆

Q. What is the nation's largest cellular telephone company?

A. McCaw Cellular Communications in Kirkland.

◆

Q. What is the name of the Northern Hemisphere's equivalent to the penguin that you can see off the Washington coast near Gray's Harbor?

A. Cassin's auklet.

◆

Q. What percentage of Whatcom County's daily collection of one hundred tons of organic garbage is made into compost at the Ferndale disposal facility?

A. 60 percent.

◆

Q. What are the first flowers to break through the snow in western Washington's alpine valleys?

A. White avalanche lilies and yellow glacier lilies.

Q. Pat Gates' invention Gateskates, which combines skating and skiing, adds what important feature the other two sports lack?

A. Brakes.

———◆———

Q. Why is the soil in the Yakima Valley twice as productive as soil elsewhere?

A. It was formed from nutrient-rich volcanic ash.

———◆———

Q. Although its motto is now Hanford—Environmental Excellence, what was the Hanford company's motto during its plutonium-producing days?

A. Hanford, a National Asset.

———◆———

Q. What Washington State University archaeologist was instrumental in proving that humans have been present in the Pacific Northwest for at least the past ten thousand years?

A. Richard Daugherty.

———◆———

Q. How many wineries are there along the Yakima River?

A. Thirteen.

———◆———

Q. What does the rare breed of monarch butterfly that lives in Moxee Bog feed on?

A. Violets.

———◆———

Q. Genuine Walla Walla sweet onions, produced only in Walla Walla and Umatilla counties, carry what guarantee?

A. They do not cause tears when chopped.

**Q.** Where is found the oldest grove of cedars (between 2,000 and 4,000 years old) in the state?

**A.** Willapa National Wildlife Refuge.

◆

**Q.** During what months do whales migrate south along the Washington coast?

**A.** November and December.

◆

**Q.** Where is a migratory bird refuge containing over three thousand acres?

**A.** Ridgefield.

◆

**Q.** Jasper, jade, geodes, opal, agate, and petrified wood are all found in what area set aside for rockhounds?

**A.** Walker Valley.

◆

**Q.** Who brought the seed stock for the Walla Walla sweet onion from Europe at the turn of the century?

**A.** Peter Pieri.

◆

**Q.** Where is the state's oldest Masonic temple located?

**A.** Port Gamble (chartered in 1859).

◆

**Q.** Who coined the phrase *flying saucer* after he saw nine shining objects near Mount Rainier in 1947?

**A.** Kenneth Boise.

Q. How many chapters of the Audubon Society are there in Washington?

A. Twenty-one.

———◆———

Q. What is the specialty of both the Silvaseed Company of Roy and the Brown Seed Company of Vancouver?

A. Cones for tree seeds.

———◆———

Q. What unusual act of equine medicine was performed by veterinarians from Washington State University?

A. They fitted a horse with an artificial leg.

———◆———

Q. On what San Juan island was marijuana, with a reputed street value of several million dollars, found growing in a greenhouse?

A. Lopez.

———◆———

Q. After the San Juans, what is the next best place in Washington to see bald eagles?

A. Marblemount Eagle Sanctuary.

———◆———

Q. What are calks?

A. Short-spiked boots used in logging.

———◆———

Q. How many different types of butterflies live in Washington?

A. 140.

**Q.** The world's largest flea (.13 inches) was found near what city?

**A.** Puyallup.

———◆———

**Q.** What ingenious device did Lou Hyatt develop?

**A.** A mechanical huckleberry picker.

———◆———

**Q.** In which Seattle lake were two caymans found in the 1980s?

**A.** Greenlake.

———◆———

**Q.** How many varieties of lilac grow in the John A. Finch Arboretum?

**A.** Fifty-seven.

———◆———

**Q.** How long does it take a Japanese fishing float to arrive by ocean currents onto a Washington beach?

**A.** About three years.

———◆———

**Q.** Where is found the largest collection of branding irons in the country?

**A.** The Asotin County Historic Museum.

———◆———

**Q.** Over the last twenty-five years, Washington has led the world in sightings of what strange creature?

**A.** Sasquatch (over 347).

Q. What woman governor was a former professor of marine zoology, U.S. assistant secretary of state for environmental and scientific affairs, and chairman of the Atomic Energy Commission?

A. Dixy Lee Ray.

———————◆———————

Q. In 1847, how did white settlers cause disaster to Indian children?

A. They brought an epidemic of measles that caused many deaths.

———————◆———————

Q. At the beginning of the twentieth century, what animals were imported to the Azwell area in an attempt to use them as pack animals?

A. Camels.

———————◆———————

Q. What was special about the 1991 Washington apple harvest?

A. It was the largest in the state's history (more than one billion dollars).

———————◆———————

Q. What community in Washington will have had three total solar eclipses in less than one hundred years?

A. Goldendale.

———————◆———————

Q. What telephone device is illegal in Washington?

A. Automatic dialers that dial a number and play a tape.

———————◆———————

Q. What two hot springs on the Olympic Peninsula are said to be the tears wept by two lightning fish?

A. The Sol Duc and the Olympic.

Q. How many glaciers in Washington contain ice worms?

A. Fifteen.

———◆———

Q. Where was found the world's largest known tree fungus (over 300 pounds)?

A. Mt. Rainier National Park (in 1946).

———◆———

Q. Where is the highest concentration of wintering loons in North America?

A. In the San Juan Islands.

———◆———

Q. What distinction does the banana slug hold?

A. It is the only slug native to the Northwest.

Patricia Hedtke owns and operates COSPRO, a private research and technical consulting firm. John V. Hedtke has written a number of computer books, including the award-winning *Using Bulletin Boards*, and does technical communications consulting. Patricia and John live in Seattle, where it rains most of the time.